WORLD BANK WORKING PAPER NO. 75

Economic Cooperation in the Wider Central Asia Region

William Byrd
Martin Raiser

With
Anton Dobronogov
Alexander Kitain

THE WORLD BANK
Washington, D.C.

ISBN-10: 0-8213-6601-7   ISBN-13: 978-0-8213-6601-1
eISBN: 0-8213-6602-5
ISSN: 1726-5878   DOI: 10.1596/978-0-8213-6601-1

William Byrd is an Adviser in the Poverty Reducation and Economic Management Unit in the South
Asia Region of the World Bank. Martin Raiser is Country Manager in the Tashkent office of the World
Bank. Anton Dobronogov is a Country Economist in the Social and Economic Development Group of
the Middle East and North Africa Region of the World Bank. Alexander Kitain is Consultant in the
Poverty Reducation and Economic Management Unit in the South Asia Region of the World Bank.

Library of Congress Cataloging-in-Publication Data has been requested.

Contents

LIST OF FIGURES

LIST OF BOXES

Acknowledgments

An earlier version of this paper was presented at the Kabul Conference on Regional Economic Cooperation (December 3–5, 2005). The paper was prepared by a World Bank team led by William Byrd (South Asia Region) and Martin Raiser (Europe and Central Asia Region) and also including Anton Dobronogov (Middle East and North Africa Region) and Alexander Kitain (Consultant). Inputs and comments were received from a number of World Bank staff including Masood Ahmad, Anna Bjerde, Amer Durrani, Julia Fraser, Stephane Guimbert, Simon Kenny, Raghuveer Sharma, Vladislav Vucetic, and Michel Zarnowiecki. The paper was prepared under the overall guidance of Dennis de Tray, Alastair McKechnie, and Joseph Saba (World Bank Country Directors in ECA, SAR, and MNA, respectively), and supervision was provided by Sadiq Ahmed and Ijaz Nabi (Sector Director and Sector Manager, respectively, SASPR). The paper was processed by Juliet Teodosio. The findings, interpretations, and conclusions expressed in the paper are those of the authors and should not be attributed in any matter to the World Bank, to its affiliated organizations, or to members of its Board of Executive Directors or the countries they represent.

Executive Summary

Background

Central Asia has had a turbulent history, sometimes as a "land bridge" for trade and ideas between the world's main civilizations, but since the 19th century increasingly fragmented—the locus of fault lines between major powers surrounding the region. Starting with the breakup of the former Soviet Union and more recently the overthrow of the Taliban regime and end of major conflict in Afghanistan, opportunities have opened up for regional cooperation, with the potential to benefit all of the countries of the region. Although there has been some development of trade and other economic interactions, driven to a large extent by the dynamic informal private sector active in the region, opportunities for more systematic regional cooperation and development have not been substantially exploited. This reflects the legacy of conflicts, continuing security concerns, infrastructural and administrative constraints, differing geopolitical conceptions for the region, and differing degrees of openness and private sector orientation among countries. Opportunities for quick "win-win" solutions appear to be relatively few, and thus concerted efforts are needed to prioritize and exploit them.

The countries of the region share many economic characteristics (much of the region landlocked, difficult terrain and underdeveloped infrastructure, legacy of public sector involvement in the economy, a vibrant informal private sector). However, there is also considerable diversity (in economic size, level of development, energy and water endowments, trade regimes and economic policy regimes, and so forth). While diversity in resource endowments and economic structures can be a source of gains from trade (with countries exporting to each other on the basis of comparative advantage), diversity can also be an impediment to closer interactions. For example, differing endowments of water resources could lead to disputes among riparian countries, divergence in per capita incomes could trigger significant cross-border labor movements, and differences in trade regimes hinder trade and drive it underground. Moreover, limited government capacity, weak governance, and corruption create additional impediments for private business in the region, drive it into the informal sector, and further limit and distort economic exchange.

The wider Central Asia region (see definition in footnote 1 on page 1) includes and is surrounded by several important regional powers and has considerable geopolitical importance. Unfortunately, regional and global rivalries in the recent past tended to hold the region back and have fomented instability and violence. This provides an important, if sobering, background for greater regional cooperation. The prospects for turning the wider Central Asia region once again into a land bridge on the Eurasian continent will thus depend on collaboration not just among the countries of the region themselves, but among the region's important neighbors as well. A number of regional groupings exist, which to varying extents include neighboring powers and could be harnessed as vehicles for greater cooperation.

Objectives and Approach

This paper has a two-fold purpose: (1) to lay out the big issues that affect regional cooperation and development in the wider Central Asia region, focusing on the critical interrelationships among these issues; and (2) to analyze in greater detail selected areas where there appear to be good prospects for progress in the short run, and which may help generate momentum and facilitate "breakthroughs" in dealing with more difficult issues. The paper is not comprehensive and, in the interest of achieving focus, has left out, or not discussed in detail, a number of important issues. Additional areas may be the subject of future analytical work.

The framework for approaching regional cooperation developed in this paper is based on two fundamental analytical findings:

- *Critical linkages among sectors:* The following have been identified: (i) between border management, security, narcotics, labor movements, and trade and transit facilitation; (ii) between transport infrastructure and trade and transport facilitation; (iii) between narcotics production and trafficking, irrigation investments and water allocation along the major river basins, and regional labor movements; and (iv) between electricity trade, hydropower generation, and water issues.
- *Political obstacles to progress and corresponding need for political incentives:* The track record on regional cooperation has been modest to date, reflecting the strength of the obstacles noted above—in part physical and financial but to a large extent political. Rather than frontal attacks on political obstacles that may have little chance of success in the short run, the paper suggests a two-pronged approach: (i) in the short term the focus should be on "win-win" initiatives that aim to build mutual confidence and ease political concerns; and (ii) these initiatives should be complemented by a few selected "bold strokes" where donor support could help increase and alter the distribution of benefits from regional cooperation in ways that make a visible breakthrough possible. Both approaches would help build the basis for more far-reaching and institutionalized regional cooperation and associated domestic reforms in the future.

To move forward with this agenda, the paper advocates that governments and partners in the region should, first, keep the "big picture" issues of regional cooperation and development in mind, including the linkages among them and the obstacles. Second, governments and partners should identify and agree on areas where there are good possibilities for near-term success (based on mutually beneficial, less controversial projects) and which may serve as entry points for further progress. Third, prioritized, intensive work (including further analysis to robustly establish estimated benefits) is needed on these few selected areas, with regular monitoring of progress and feedback to decisionmakers. Some of the existing regional organizations, if revitalized, may be able to play such a monitoring and feedback role. Fourth, capacity building will be essential, most notably in the case of Afghanistan but also in some of the other regional countries and in some of the regional organizations. Finally, it must be recognized that opportunities for progress are unlikely to be spread evenly throughout the region but will often involve subgroups of countries and sometimes bilateral cooperation between different pairings of countries. Such opportunities should be exploited and may themselves encourage similar initiatives involving other regional countries. However, in some areas—such as harmonization of customs procedures, visa policies, border management initiatives, transit standards, and so forth—there are important advantages to coordinated regional initiatives so these should be pursued as is already occurring in some cases.

Electricity Trade

Perhaps the greatest prospects for quick win-win initiatives at the regional level are in electricity trade. Afghanistan's power needs, and donors' willingness to fund investments in transmission infrastructure, create electricity export opportunities for neighboring countries. Successful exploitation of such opportunities for bilateral trade in electricity will build a track record of cooperation and momentum for larger-scale initiatives. There are also possibilities for one or more "bold stroke" projects with large benefits for a number of regional countries and significant private sector participation. Progress with these initiatives may open up prospects over the medium term for developing a regional power market, with major electricity flows and benefits. Specific recommendations include:

- *Formalize power trading agreements* between Afghanistan and neighbors where appropriate (that is, there is mutual agreement for stable multi-year trade).
- *Accelerate construction of critical transmission infrastructure* to ensure that this does not become a bottleneck to expanding electricity trade, where a bilateral or multilateral agreement to trade power exists.
- *Conduct a study on regional energy markets* that includes all countries in the wider Central Asia region, building on the Regional Energy Export Potential Study for post-Soviet Central Asia, and fully in line with the analytical work envisaged by ECO.
- *Solicit private sector interest* in longer-term investments in generation and transmission systems, focusing first on run of the river hydel opportunities and thermal generation.
- *Continue developing an institutional framework* within which longer-term issues of energy development and trade, and possible integration of electricity markets, can be discussed and resolved.

Transport Development

The potential gains from regional cooperation in the transport sector are large but unequally distributed both within and between countries. Hence quick win solutions will require a greater degree of political buy-in and leadership from the governments in the region, as well as selectivity and focus by donors in order to leverage their financial support. Perhaps the best chance for achieving multilateral progress lies in establishing performance benchmarks to highlight the urgency and the benefits of action. It may also be possible to identify particular transport corridors where the benefits of cooperation could be clearly demonstrated. Donors should structure their assistance in a way that maximizes these opportunities. In the meantime, national trade facilitation policies and bilateral agreements should be designed in ways that would fit easily into a wider regional approach. External anchors such as the WTO accession process or existing regional cooperation organizations could be used to coordinate national policies. Investments to rehabilitate transport corridors need to be sequenced in ways that are coordinated among different donors along major routes, and which recognize and reward countries for demonstrated progress in trade facilitation. As a way of generating additional pressure, transport routes bypassing countries that are dragging their feet on trade facilitation and economic cooperation should be costed and may be considered for donor funding. Specific recommendations include:

- ▓ *Undertake a review of existing transportation routes to identify particular bottle-necks* and coordinate donor assistance for physical reconstruction to focus on such bottlenecks.
- ▓ *Carry out a complete review of inter-regional transit routes* by calculating current and anticipated future costs of inter-continental transit corridors through Central Asia. Identify selected corridors where cooperation on a pilot basis would demonstrate benefits quickly.
- ▓ *Develop carefully sequenced investments in the sector* to leverage improvements in bilateral or multi-lateral regulations affecting trade and transit. Opportunities for "bold strokes" may exist where investments in critical infrastructure could help unlock greater policy coordination.
- ▓ *Progressively open up regional air transportation markets.*

Trade Facilitation

The trade facilitation agenda for the region is long. The liberalization of trade policies is politically sensitive for some countries, and on a region-wide basis most likely will be a longer-term endeavor. However, individual countries which have liberalized their trade regimes and those which are currently doing so should be encouraged to continue and deepen the trade liberalization process. Current trade policies and restrictions do not effectively protect the domestic markets of countries with restrictive trade regimes but simply push trade and people movements into the informal sector. One short-term measure suggested by the paper in this regard is creation of cross-border zones relating to countries with more restrictive trade regimes, where goods and people can move more freely. This would generate new employment opportunities for the poor in border areas, and would also help separate out informal trade in goods from narcotics and crime by creating incentives for informal traders to declare their products. Border guards and customs officials would be better able to concentrate on stopping criminals and controlling large cargo, rather than dissipating efforts and resources interacting with small individual traders.

Additional short-term recommendations for trade facilitation include:

- ▓ *Create a performance measurement system for border stations and transit corridors,* so that progress in improving their performance can be transparently assessed, with feedback about problems so that they can be addressed.
- ▓ *Harmonize primary legislation for customs as well as documentation requirements* in each country, in line with the Kyoto Convention and WTO.
- ▓ *Improve coordination between border enforcement agencies at the national level,* for example, through the creation of a National Trade Facilitation Council, as has been done in Pakistan.
- ▓ *Increase bilateral border management cooperation,* such as data exchanges, mutual recognition of customs documentation, and so forth. Bilateral cooperation, and donor support to customs and other border institutions, should be designed in ways that allow for easy extension to other countries.

▓ *Consider establishing a truck modernization fund with donor assistance,* which would help upgrade national fleets to meet minimum performance standards, subject to concrete measures by regional countries to reduce entry barriers for trucks from neighboring countries, such as truck entry bans or fees, convoy requirements for transit trucks even under TIR, and cumbersome visa requirements for truckers.

Additional proposals, which may require more time, include the following:

▓ *Enforce the TIR convention among post-Soviet countries* and consider the establishment of a temporary alternative transit insurance system for the rest of wider Central Asia.

▓ *Create one common visa zone for all post-Soviet Central Asian countries* (for instance in the context of EurASEC) and reduce visa fees for non-CIS members.

▓ *Create a regional association of transport operators* to lobby for improved regulation and enforce a self-policing regime.

The paper also offers some short-term recommendations relating to *water issues,* as well as the *security–border management–narcotics–labor movements* nexus, but the resolution of larger regional issues in these areas is likely to be politically sensitive and difficult, and will probably take more time. Nevertheless, the proposed initiatives will help pave the way for further progress when that becomes possible. Specific recommendations include the following:

▓ *Concerted efforts to measure water flows and use in Afghanistan,* for which the information base is very weak.

▓ *Accelerated rehabilitation of existing water conservancy facilities in Afghanistan,* which does not raise riparian issues.

▓ *Participation by Afghanistan in existing riparian groups,* specifically for the Amu Darya; this could initially be on a special basis if there is no existing agreement.

▓ *Initiation/continuation of technical-level dialogue* between Iran and Afghanistan with respect to the Helmand River and between Pakistan and Afghanistan with respect to the Kabul River.

▓ *Technical work on improving water utilization,* which can benefit all regional countries.

▓ *Develop pilot schemes for cross-border movement of goods and people within a limited border zone* to formalize existing informal movements.

▓ *Ensure adequate donor assistance to border guards* to fight against the drug trade, perhaps concentrated initially on a few pilot border posts along major trade and transit routes, to demonstrate how security concerns and trade facilitation can be simultaneously addressed.

▓ *Develop bilateral agreements on temporary migration and sharing of border facilities.*

Conclusions

Governments of the countries of the wider Central Asia region may be encouraged to cooperate with each other in the awareness of the important linkages between sectors, of the political constraints that they are facing themselves, and therefore of the need for careful sequencing of measures to achieve maximum impact and progress over time.

Acknowledging explicitly what will be politically possible and what is unlikely to be possible in the short run would be a first confidence-building measure. Where certain countries are demonstrating unwillingness to engage in regional cooperation in important areas of mutual benefit, the other countries who are interested in moving forward may start exploring second-best solutions, bypassing countries that refuse to enter into a substantive dialogue on regional cooperation. Such solutions ultimately would attract donor funding. It is hoped that all regional countries will recognize the benefits of greater regional cooperation and—through short-term measures along the lines suggested here—progressively build the trust and momentum that will make such bypass solutions unnecessary.

Finally, it should be emphasized that the analysis and proposals in this paper are preliminary and are intended to generate further discussion and consideration. Above all, these issues, and the proposals for entry points and ways forward, need to be carefully considered by the regional countries themselves. The concrete ideas are perhaps less important than the analytical framework and overall approach put forward in the paper.

CHAPTER 1

Introduction

This paper has a two-fold purpose: (1) to lay out some big issues that affect regional cooperation and development in the wider Central Asia region,[1] focusing in particular on the critical interrelationships among these issues; and (2) to analyze in greater detail selected areas where there appear to be good prospects for progress in the short run, and which may help generate momentum and facilitate "breakthroughs" in dealing with more difficult issues.

This first chapter provides some historical background, briefly summarizes the common features and diversity of the economies of the region, and discusses geopolitical and political economy considerations. Chapter 2 provides a sector-by-sector overview of the main issues for regional development: (i) security, border management, narcotics, and people movements and regional labor markets; (ii) transport connections and infrastructure; (iii) prospects and constraints for development of regional and transit trade; (iv) prospects for energy development and trade; and (v) water issues.

Following this overview of the "big picture" issues in each of these areas, the paper suggests selected areas where prospects for moving ahead with regional cooperation in a timely manner appear to be good, based on: (i) technical feasibility—can be implemented taking into account weak capacity especially in Afghanistan; (ii) high economic returns, shared

---

1. The definition of a "Central Asia Region" is somewhat arbitrary and varies with the countries and organizations that are making the definition. Moreover, geography is such that a number of countries (or at least parts of their territories) fall into more than one geographical or geopolitical cluster. For the purpose of this study, the wider Central Asia region is defined to include Afghanistan, Kazakhstan, Kyrgyz Republic, Tajikistan, Turkmenistan, Uzbekistan, and, at least in terms of parts of their territories and strong economic ties, Iran, Pakistan and, for the post-Soviet states of Central Asia, Russia. Of major importance for the wider Central Asia region are a set of large neighboring countries/areas including China, India, and the Middle East.

among countries ("win-win"); (iii) manageable in terms of geopolitical and political economy considerations; and (iv) policy framework to realize benefits in place or has reasonable prospects of being put in place. The paper adopts a pragmatic approach in looking for ways to create momentum behind regional cooperation, suggesting small steps that could build trust and change the perceptions of political leaders, but also highlighting areas where "bold strokes" are possible—sizable projects with high impact, high visibility, and where donor financing might be critical for achieving a breakthrough. The main recommendations for action in the short run are listed at the end of each sectoral analysis in Chapter 2. More detailed background notes which motivate these recommendations are included as Appendixes on cooperation in the electricity sector (Appendix A), regional transportation links (Appendix B), and trade and transit facilitation (Appendix C). Chapter 3 concludes the paper with some general observations and recommendations for moving forward in the short run focused on these three sectors.

It should be emphasized at the outset that this paper is not comprehensive and has left out, or not discussed in any detail, a number of important issues, such as financial flows in the region, trade in services, standards, public sector procurement, participation of regional countries in reconstruction activities in Afghanistan, direct foreign investment, the hydrocarbon sector, regional agricultural issues, environment, and so forth. This is in the interest of achieving focus. Additional areas may be the subject of future analytical work, depending on demand and their importance from a regional perspective.

Historical Background

Central Asia has had a turbulent history, both internally and as a field for competition and conflict among empires and major powers. On certain occasions the region has been a "land bridge" for trade and ideas, bringing different parts of the Eurasian landmass and its civilizations closer together. More recently it has been the locus of fault lines between different powers as they ran into their military and political limits in the face of the mountainous topography and fiercely independent peoples of the region. As a result, since the 19th century the wider Central Asia region has been fragmented—becoming a region of barriers and conflicts rather than economic and people-to-people connections.

Changing geopolitical circumstances, starting with the break-up of the former Soviet Union in the early 1990s and more recently with the overthrow of the Taliban regime and the end of major conflict in Afghanistan, have opened up opportunities for regional economic cooperation, which potentially can benefit all of the countries of the region. Several neighboring and nearby countries are supporting Afghanistan's reconstruction with financial and technical assistance. Progress has been made in the development of trade and other economic interactions among some of the countries. To date such integration has been driven to a large extent by the dynamic informal private sector that is active in the region. Despite a number of regional meetings, however, opportunities for more systematic regional cooperation and development have not been substantially exploited.

This lack of concrete progress reflects, among other constraints, the legacy of conflicts, continuing security concerns, infrastructural and administrative constraints, differing geopolitical conceptions for the region, and differing degrees of openness and private sector orientation in the economic policy regimes of the regional countries. The fact that five of the countries in the region only recently gained sovereignty is an additional political constraint that needs to be borne in mind, as it has motivated attempts to become also economically independent, even if at considerable cost. One conclusion of this paper is that in the face of these constraints, the opportunities for rapid win-win solutions are relatively few. Thus efforts to encourage greater regional cooperation will need to be focused on a few priority areas.

The Economies of the Region

Most countries in the wider Central Asia region share some common economic characteristics, such as difficult terrain and lack of direct access to the sea, underdeveloped transport infrastructure, and a largely commodity-oriented structure of exports (Table 1.1). Many of the countries (although not all of them) have a legacy of substantial public sector involvement in their economies but at the same time face significant constraints in administrative capacity. There are also significant cultural and ethnic ties across many of the countries, even if these have at times been ruptured by the experience of conflict and geopolitical rivalries.

One of the defining characteristics of the region is the vibrant informal sector, which means that in most cases unofficial economic ties are stronger than formal economic relationships among the countries. Informal trade—often called "shuttle trade" or unofficial trade—is common, involving usually small-scale movement of goods across countries on an unofficial basis. Dubai, where the business climate is excellent for private sector activity on a virtually "free-trade" basis, serves as an economic hub for large parts of the region.[2] Chinese consumer goods are increasingly present in the markets of the region, brought in by individual traders on land routes through Kazakhstan and the Kyrgyz Republic. Informal traders take advantage of arbitrage opportunities offered by the widely diverging trade regimes in the region, thereby mitigating the distortionary effects of the more restrictive trade regimes. More organized, larger-scale informal trade also is prevalent in major protected markets such as Pakistan and Uzbekistan. While the informal sector provides a vital source of income for many poor people in the region, it also presents some drawbacks for governments. Tax and customs collection suffers, and security risks associated with the uncontrolled movement of goods and people are a concern. The informal sector can also be a constraint on longer-term growth, as it relies on personal or kin connections and has limited access to finance; moreover, informal sector business entities tend not to expand in size beyond a certain point, don't modernize their technology, and face difficulties breaking into export markets. A key challenge therefore, and a theme to which this paper returns repeatedly, is to create incentives for the formalization of economic exchange rather than attempting to repress informal exchange of legal goods through additional controls.[3]

---

2. Even in post-Soviet Central Asia, for instance, informal trade with Dubai is relatively well developed. The price margins for goods such as consumer electronics and other durables are often high enough to cover the cost of a plane ticket, and there are flights between Dubai and capital cities in Central Asia almost on a daily basis.

3. For an analysis of Afghanistan's reconstruction effort which stresses this theme see World Bank (2005a). This report roughly estimates that the informal sector currently accounts for 80–90 percent of economic activity in Afghanistan.

Table 1.1. Basic Economic Data on Wider Central Asia (WCA) and its Main Neighbors (2004)

Country	Population (millions)	GDP per Capita (US $)	Total GDP (US$ billion)	Agriculture in GDP (% of GDP)	Exports (US$ billion)	Imports (US$ billion)	Primary Energy (oil, gas, coal)/a (MTOE)	Exploitable Hydro Power Potential/a (TWh/year)	Literacy Rate (%)
Afghanistan	24	c. 250	6/b	52	–/c	–	–	–	c. 30
Kazakhstan	15	2724	41	7	18	16	27914	62	93
Kyrgyz Republic	5	432	2	39	1	1	591	99	92
Tajikistan	6	323	2	24	1	1	507	317	90
Turkmenistan	5	1251	6	25	4	3	2684	5	93
Uzbekistan	26	461	12	35	5	4	4606	27	91
Subtotal Central Asian countries:	81	5441	69	182	29	25	36302	510	489
Iran	67	2431	163	11	38	36	42818	88	77
Pakistan	152	632	96	23	15	15	1735	130	49
Russia	143	4078	582	5	177	123	121758	1670	95
Subtotal WCA	443	12582	910	221	259	199	202613	2398	710
China	1296	1272	1649	15	639	624	63234	1920	90
India	1080	638	689	22	112	124	62433	660	61
Turkey	72	4210	302	12	91	102	1488	216	88
UAE	4	23810	102/e	22	82/e	54/e	18794	–	77
Total for WCA plus main neighbors	2895	42512	3550	292	1101	1049	348562	5194	1026

Notes: China is placed in the group of main neighbors countries, because although it borders on Afghanistan and other Central Asian countries, it is a major global economy for which economic relations with Wider Central Asia comprise only a relatively small portion of its total economic activity.
a. The data on technically exploitable capacity came from World Energy Council (Survey of Energy Resources)
b. Not including opium economy.
c. It should be noted that a blank (i.e. "–") does not mean zero; data for these items/countries were not immediately available.
d. Totals do not include countries for which information is not available, notably Afghanistan.
e. Latest available data from U.S. Department of State.
Source: Data are for 2004 or latest year available data from World Bank (Central and Regional databases), unless otherwise indicated.

Just as striking as the common features is the considerable diversity across countries in the region. As shown in Table 1.1, there is great diversity in economic size (population and total GDP), level of development (per capita GDP as well as human capital, proxied by the literacy rate), and economic structure (for example, share of agriculture in GDP). Energy endowments vary considerably across the regional countries, in terms of both amounts and types of energy resources, and there are also great differences in endowments of water, the scarce resource in the region.

While diversity in resource endowments and economic structures can be a source of gains from trade (with countries exporting to each other on the basis of comparative advantage), diversity may also in some respects constitute an impediment to closer economic interactions. For instance, differing endowments of water resources could be a source of disputes, particularly given the riparian relationships among many of the countries. Divergence in per capita incomes could trigger significant cross-border labor movements, which while economically beneficial may be a source of political tension for security and other reasons.

There is also considerable diversity within the region in terms of economic policy regimes (Table 1.2). For example, the countries vary greatly in terms of trade restrictiveness, with overall ratings ranging from the least restrictive rating of "1" to just one level below the most restrictive rating of "10." While differing resource endowments and economic structures create potential for gains from trade, widely differing economic policy regimes constitute an impediment to closer economic cooperation, most notably in the

Table 1.2. Governance and Economic Policy Regimes

	Political Stability Index	Rule of Law Index	Control of Corruption	Overall Trade Restrictiveness Index	Non-Tariff Barriers Index	Average Import Tariff (%)
Wider CA Region:						
Afghanistan	3.4	1	3.9	4	2	5.3
Iran	19.9	23.2	35	7	2	22.7
Kazakhstan	45.6	17.4	9.9	4	2	7.4
Kyrgyz Republic	19.9	15	15.3	1	1	5.2
Pakistan	6.3	26.1	20.2	6	2	16.5
Russia	21.8	29.5	29.1	5	2	11.1
Tajikistan	13.1	9.2	8.9	1	1	7.6
Turkmenistan	18.9	5.8	3.4	7	3	5.6
Uzbekistan	9.7	7.7	5.9	9	3	14.6
Main Neighbors:						
China	46.6	40.6	39.9	5	2	10.5
India	24.3	50.7	47.3	7	2	22.0
Turkey	30.6	54.6	50.7	5	2	12.7
UAE	78.2	78.7	86.7	1	1	5.0

Source: Political Stability Index, Rule of Law Index, Corruption Index: Kaufman, Kraay, and Mastruzzi (2005), shown in percentiles of countries. It should be noted that as they are based on polls and surveys, these indexes have significant margins of error, reflected in the standard errors reported in the source.
Trade restrictions: IMF Trade Policy Information Database.

case of intra-regional trade. Moreover, limited government capacity, weak governance, and corruption create additional impediments for private business in the region, drive it into the informal sector, and further limit and distort economic exchange.

It is interesting to note that trade within the Central Asia region constitutes only a small fraction of the region's total trade, while when the other wider Central Asia countries and main neighbors are added, this proportion rises to well over 50 percent of total trade (Appendix B). This pattern of trade suggests that there would be significant welfare gains from reducing the costs of trade between wider Central Asia and its large neighbors. It also suggests that a large share of trade in the region may be affected by geopolitical considerations relating to regional and surrounding countries (see the discussion that follows).

Current Geopolitical and Political Economy Considerations

The wider Central Asia region includes and is surrounded by a number of important regional powers. To the North, Russia has since the 17th century exercised increasingly significant control over the region, colonizing the area down to the Amu Darya River and during Soviet rule extending its occupation into Afghanistan. In the southern part of the region, Pakistan since its birth in 1947 has had special interests in and close economic relations with Afghanistan. From the subcontinent, India is an important geopolitical player for the region, with important and growing economic relationships. In the West, Iran has both traditional cultural ties with other countries in the region (including a common language with Afghanistan and Tajikistan) and is becoming an important economic partner to some of the countries. Further to the west, Turkey has cultural and economic ties with Central Asia. And to the East, China's growing economic power is increasingly reflected in expanding trade and investment relations with wider Central Asia, and China also has declared strategic and security interests in the region. More distantly, Japan is an important donor to all Central Asian countries and has stressed the importance of regional cooperation. Finally, Europe—in particular the UK—and America have played an important role, initially the former as a colonial power, then as sponsors of the anti-Soviet resistance in Afghanistan, as investors in Caspian energy resources, and after 9/11 as military actors and key sponsors of Afghanistan's reconstruction.

The Central Asia region thus is indeed unique in lying at the frontiers of influence of the world's major economic and military powers. Unfortunately their rivalries have in the recent past tended to hold the region back and have fomented instability and violence. The legacy of these rivalries and conflicts persists to some extent today and forms an important, if sobering, background to the prospects for greater regional cooperation:

■ During the Cold War, Afghanistan preserved its neutrality for a long period of time but eventually was occupied by the Soviet Union and became one of the victims of the Soviet-western confrontation, which accentuated domestic divisions that are only gradually being overcome.

■ While in Afghanistan distrust of Russia to some extent persists, conversely the experience of Taliban rule has created significant unease in post-Soviet Central Asia and in Russia itself about the dangers of imported Islamist political and security challenges from the South. Further, Afghanistan has concerns about support for the continuing insurgency in parts of the country by interests in Pakistan.

▧ Iran is locked in a diplomatic dispute with the international community over its nuclear program, which may have uncertain consequences for Iran's role in the region. U.S. firms are currently banned from doing business in Iran.

▧ Central Asia's strategic location and in particular its large energy resources are a source of competition between Russia, China, and the West. Such competition can stimulate development, but when political tactics include blocking rival transit solutions, the region suffers.

▧ Relations between India and Pakistan have traditionally been difficult. The attractiveness of a southern transit and export route from Central Asia depends to a considerable extent on successfully managing historical rivalries between these two countries.

The prospects of turning the wider Central Asia region once again into a land bridge on the Eurasian continent will thus depend on collaboration not just among the countries of the region themselves, but among the region's important neighbors as well. A number of regional groupings already exist, which to varying extents include the region's neighboring powers and could be harnessed as vehicles for greater cooperation (Table 1.3).

Table 1.3. Regional Agreements Involving Wider Central Asia and its Neighbors

	CACO	CAREC	CIS	CSATTF	ECO	EurASEC	SAARC	ShOS	SPECA
CA Region:									
Afghanistan		X		X	X		(X)		
Kazakhstan	X	X	X		X	X		X	X
Kyrgyz Republic	X	X	X		X	X		X	X
Tajikistan	X	X	X	X	X	X		X	X
Turkmenistan				X	X				X
Uzbekistan	X	X	X	X	X	(X)		X	X
Other WCA countries:									
Iran				X	X			O	
Pakistan				X	X		X	O	
Russia	X	(X)	X			X		X	
Main WCA Neighbors:									
China		X					(O)	X	
India							X	O	
Turkey					X				
UAE									

Legend: X = member; (X) = membership under consideration; O = observer; (O) = observer status under consideration
CACO   = Central Asian Cooperation Organization (a successor of CAEC since 2002)
CAREC   = Central Asia Regional Economic Cooperation
CIS   = Commonwealth of Independent States
CSATTF   = Central and South Asia Transport and Trade Forum
ECO   = Economic Cooperation Organization, formed in 1996
EurASEC   = EurASian Economic Community (known as the Union of Five until 2000)
SAARC   = South Asian Association for Regional Cooperation
ShOS   = Shanghai Organization for Security and Cooperation (Shanghai Five with Uzbekistan)
SPECA   = Special Programme for the Economies of Central Asia, launched in 1998
Source: World Bank staff based on available information.

Five recent developments deserve particular attention. First, the recent application of Uzbekistan for membership in EurASEC and the consequent merger of CACO with the former raise the prospect that the considerable policy barriers to greater cooperation among the post-Soviet republics of Central Asia might be addressed finally. An economically more integrated post-Soviet Central Asia would be far more attractive as a region for both exporters and investors, creating significant additional potential for transit through Afghanistan. Second, the growing membership of the Shanghai Organization for Security and Cooperation (ShoS), which Iran, India, and Pakistan have joined as observers, and its growing focus on economic cooperation in addition to security matters, could create a regional body encompassing all of the region's major neighbors. This could provide a chance to address issues of harmonizing trade and transit policies, and coordinating large regional investments in transport infrastructure. Third, with Afghanistan and (potentially) Russia joining the CAREC process, this group, which coordinates IFI and donor assistance and has been a key vehicle for pushing ahead with policy coordination in post-Soviet Central Asia, now has a chance to extend its work further along the North-South axis. Fourth, the SAARC Summit in November 2005 agreed to admit Afghanistan as a member of SAARC and discussed the possibility of China gaining observer status. Fifth, Afghanistan has just initiated the WTO accession process. All of these developments are positive from the perspective of enhancing regional cooperation but will need to be followed up to build and sustain momentum.

CHAPTER 2

Main Challenges and Prospects for Regional Cooperation

This chapter provides an overview of the main areas and key issues that will be important for regional cooperation. First it highlights some "critical clusters" of major issues that are impeding regional cooperation and development, which will require innovative and well-sequenced actions to address over time. Building on this thematic overview, the section looks at the closely-interlinked nexus of security, border management, narcotics issues, and cross-border people movements and regional labor markets. The chapter then analyzes the prospects for increased regional and longer-distance transit trade through investments in transportation corridors. This is followed by an analysis of the policy obstacles to greater trade and transit, which will dictate the extent to which new investments in transportation infrastructure are economically justified. Prospects for energy development and trade are then summarized along with the constraints, and the section closes with a discussion of water issues. In each case, the summary of sectoral issues is followed by some short-run recommendations, which are taken up in more detail for selected sectors in the three Appendixes.

Thematic Overview

There are good medium-term prospects in the wider Central Asia region for regional economic cooperation to achieve expansion of regional trade and possibly also long-distance transit trade, coordinated development of regional resources most notably energy and water, expanding electricity trade, and more generally private sector investments and robust growth of economic activity throughout the region. However, the legacy of conflicts and barriers, as well as geographical and infrastructural constraints, policy differences, institutional weaknesses, capacity limitations, geopolitical issues, and in some cases political economy interests, make it far from certain that these regional potentials will be successfully exploited. The lack of major progress so far in most areas demonstrates that the constraints and obstacles are indeed strong.

The key to unlocking the potential for regional economic cooperation and development is achieving meaningful results and selected breakthroughs in areas where progress is possible and sets in motion a dynamic whereby regional cooperation can be progressively expanded and deepened over time. More specifically, creative and effective ways must be found to make inroads on several critical, closely interrelated clusters of issues which are holding back progress. These include, most notably:

- ■ *The nexus of border security issues with narcotics, trade facilitation, and people movements.* Most countries in the region are concerned about border security and people movements because of the massive flows of opiates from Afghanistan through the region. However, enhancing border security to alleviate these concerns may make it more difficult to facilitate trade and transport and may push more economic exchange into the informal sector. Seasonal and longer-term labor migration also acts as a safety valve for the poorest economies of the region (Afghanistan, Kyrgyz Republic, Tajikistan, and Uzbekistan), and restricting it may accentuate social tensions in the labor sending countries.
- ■ *The nexus between transport infrastructure and trade and transport facilitation.* There has been a strong emphasis on investments in transport infrastructure in the region. By far the largest reconstruction investments in Afghanistan have been in highways, and there are important transport infrastructure investments underway in other countries of the region as well. However, these investments will not reap envisaged economic benefits in the absence of genuine progress in improving trade and transport facilitation.
- ■ *The nexus of water issues (from an agricultural perspective) with narcotics and people movements.* Put most starkly, if opium production in Afghanistan is progressively reduced but rural non-opium livelihoods are not greatly enhanced through, among other things, sizable irrigation projects in Afghanistan, there will be enormous incentives for out-migration of labor from Afghanistan to neighboring countries as well as pressures to resume opium production. Thus regional issues of water, narcotics, and labor movements are closely interlinked and need to be addressed holistically.
- ■ *The nexus of electricity (hydropower) and water issues.* The wider Central Asia region's large hydropower potential creates opportunities for electricity trade, but as all of the major waterways are international, water sharing and riparian issues arise. From a more positive perspective, electricity trading may be an entry point for dealing with such water issues.

Figure 2.1 summarizes these key linkages between the main issues affecting regional cooperation. The figure suggests electricity trade as the entry point for moving toward addressing water issues (related to hydropower and subsequently irrigation as well). Border trade facilitation and border management are suggested as the entry point for moving toward addressing narcotics and people movement issues (although both issues also require actions in the destination countries), whereas further major investments in transport infra-

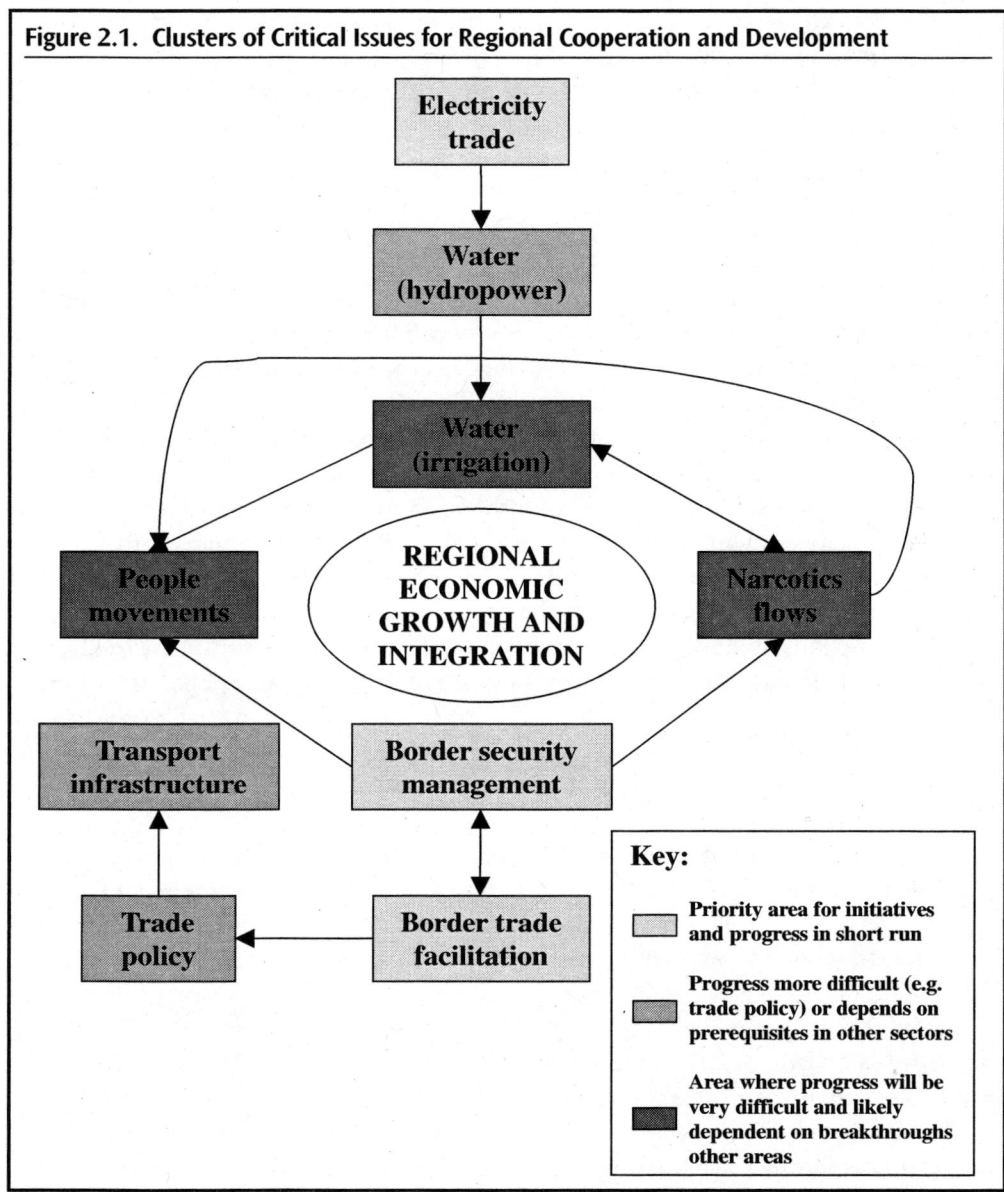

Figure 2.1. Clusters of Critical Issues for Regional Cooperation and Development

structure for the most part would be an outcome of progress on trade facilitation and trade policy, rather than vice versa.

A general theme is that exploitation of existing opportunities and "policy invest-ments," accompanied by critical quick-return (but not necessarily large) infrastructure investments, should be the priorities for focus in the short run. The need for selectivity and sequencing in this regard is obvious. Often this will require support for a series of small steps, but sometimes "bold strokes"—sizable and highly visible projects—can unlock an issue and rapidly move the agenda forward. It should also be noted that the precise sequenc-ing may differ among countries. For example, regional road infrastructure investments on a more accelerated basis may make sense in the case of countries which have relatively good trade regimes and have made progress with trade facilitation.

The themes outlined above will be drawn out further in the discussions on individual sectors in the rest of this chapter.

Security, Border Management, Narcotics, and Labor Movements

The nexus of security issues and concerns on the part of regional countries, porous borders that are not clearly defined in some places[4] and difficult to manage in many areas, and massive flows of illicit opiates through the region together constitute critical constraints impeding regional economic cooperation and development. These issues also heavily impinge on people movements and trade facilitation, which tend to be restricted due to concerns related to security and narcotics. It should be emphasized that such concerns and restrictions mainly impede formalized economic relationships—movements of people with visas, official trade flows, investments in formal-sector activities, and the like. There is a lively informal economy, especially prevalent in Afghanistan but present throughout the region, that easily makes use of porous borders and the corruptibility of officials to get around government restrictions on flows of goods, people, and money. Thus a key theme in this area is the need for risk management, through the concentration of scarce police resources on high risks, and the creation of incentives for informal economic activity to become formal.

Security

The legacy of the protracted conflicts in the region persists in the form of continuing security concerns on the part of many countries. Afghanistan, the main victim of conflict over the past several decades, is seen by some neighbors as a potential source of destabilizing Islamic fundamentalism, while Afghanistan in turn has expressed concern about support to the continuing insurgency in the southern and eastern parts of the country by interests in Pakistan. The Ferghana Valley, which runs through the Kyrgyz Republic, Tajikistan, and Uzbekistan, is a region with significant conflict potential, where radical Islamic groups have recently stepped up their presence. Uzbekistan for instance has justified tight border controls (including in earlier years the mining of border areas) based on fear of infiltration of Islamic groups through neighboring countries. Aside from these more political security concerns, there are concerns about cross-border crime as well, mainly focused around narcotics (see below), as well as human trafficking and smuggling and so forth.

Addressing these concerns will be a longer-term challenge, requiring sustained efforts to build confidence and trust among the countries, and to continue the reversal of past practices of interference particularly in Afghanistan but also in other regional countries. While continuing and deepening the process begun with the "Good Neighborliness" Agreement among regional countries signed in Kabul in December 2002 will be important,

---

4. This is the case for parts of the Afghanistan-Pakistan and China-India borders and also for some of the borders within post-Soviet Central Asia and with China. Moreover, there are several enclaves (of Kyrgyz and Kazakh territory in Uzbekistan, and of Uzbek territory in Kyrgyz Republic), which are often a cause of friction between countries.

equally important will be specific confidence-building measures in areas like border management and counternarcotics, as well as progress on economic cooperation which will give regional countries increasingly strong stakes in each other's economies and security.

Border Management

While virtually all of the regional countries are interested in strengthening border management in their mutual interest, measures taken to strengthen formal border procedures (such as issuing of visas, customs controls at border checkpoints, and so forth) are often ineffective in blocking criminal activities, while the resulting costs to formal economic activities and exchange represent a significant obstacle and drive even more transactions into the informal sector. Effective border management thus requires a risk-based approach, which combines efficient border clearing procedures for formal trade with enhanced border patrols to increase the costs for criminal activity. It is conceivable that in countries with weak government capacity, customs and other border services might even be concessioned out to the private sector, with government concentrating on security matters. However, such a risk-based approach is a particular challenge in countries where a control and police culture still dominates among border enforcement agencies. To be effective, a risk-based border management strategy also requires bilateral cooperation between border enforcement agencies,[5] and improved domestic cooperation between different enforcement agencies. One short-run proposal advocated by this paper would be to work on facilitating economic exchange just in border regions and creating incentives for informal traders to use officially authorized cross-border bazaars, thereby freeing up scarce capacity in border management to focus on genuine security risks (see the fourth section of this chapter).

Narcotics Production and Trade: A Regional and Global Problem

Afghanistan is the source of an estimated 87 percent of global illicit production of opium. Narcotics, including raw opium but increasingly in the form of heroin or morphine, flow out of Afghanistan in most directions, crossing through virtually all of the regional countries (see Figure 2.2). Drug trafficking in the region increases addiction rates, encourages organized crime, and often generates massive corruption, corroding governance. Thus, all of the countries in the region have a strong interest in curbing the opium trade. Afghanistan has developed a counternarcotics strategy based on alternative rural livelihoods, prohibiting poppy cultivation and eradicating poppy fields, and interdiction efforts against opium trading and processing. Yet, success in reducing opium production has been elusive. Some of the neighboring countries, most notably Iran, have taken very strong measures against drug trafficking but have not been able to stop the trade.

For example, trafficking of narcotics from Afghanistan is a major security issue for Iran. According to the UN, Iran has the highest rate of heroin and opium addiction in the

---

5. A recent encouraging example is improved cooperation along the Afghan-Tajik border, which has resulted in significant increases in drug seizures by Tajik border guards. Joint border facilities are being developed between Kazakhstan and the Kyrgyz Republic and between Kazakhstan and China, in both cases aimed at reducing the costs of formal trade. See for instance the latest report of the Trade and Transport Facilitation Committee of CAREC.

Figure 2.2. Illicit Narcotics Trading Routes and Seizures in 2001

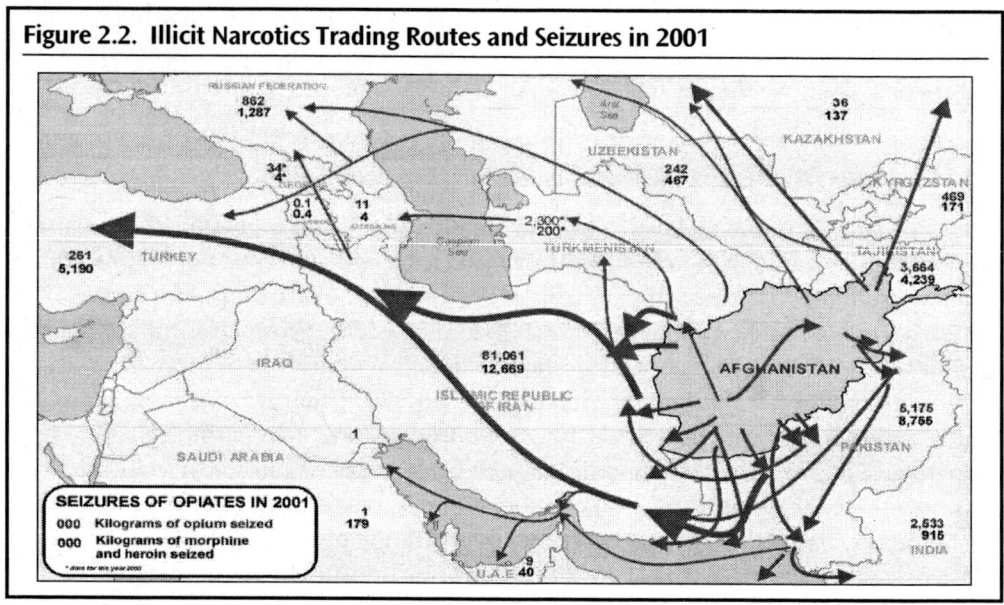

Source: UNODC (2003), p. 154.

world: about 20 percent of the Iranian population aged 15–60 are involved in drug abuse, and about 6 percent are regular drug users. According to the government's estimates, illegal drugs turnover amounted to $1.2 billion in 2004. Afghanistan is the source of Iran's narcotics imports (directly and indirectly via Pakistan). In 2003, Iran's law enforcement agencies seized 220 tons of drugs, up 54 percent from the previous year. Numerous Iranian police have been killed in gun battles with narco-gangs. Similar security risks are clearly present in Tajikistan, Turkmenistan, the Kyrgyz Republic, and to perhaps a somewhat lesser extent in Uzbekistan. Data on drug abuse and drug seizures in these countries are incomplete, but in Tajikistan, for example, the drug trade may be equivalent to up to half of total economic activity.

While closer cooperation in law enforcement against drugs (including through border management) makes good sense, the wider economic implications of the drug industry especially in Afghanistan need to be fully taken into account. Global historical experience suggests that success in eliminating or at least sharply reducing narcotics production in one country has not reduced global production on a sustained basis—production instead tends to shift to other countries with weak governance and other conditions conducive to narcotics production. Without measures to reduce demand in the destination markets and to attack the global drug trade, there is an obvious risk that success in reducing illicit opium production in Afghanistan would merely result in "displacement" of production elsewhere, possibly to one or more nearby countries in the wider Central Asia region. Moreover, as emphasized earlier, sharply reducing opium cultivation in Afghanistan without viable alternative livelihoods will exacerbate pressures for out-migration of labor from Afghanistan in search of livelihoods in neighboring countries.

Finally, experience in Afghanistan strongly suggests that going after drug traders and processors (interdiction) as opposed a primary focus on small farmers (eradication) is necessary to make sustained progress. Some successes have been achieved along the

Tajik-Afghan border, as reflected in rising drug seizures, and also in Iran, but the fight against the organized drug trade will be difficult and will require significant and sustained donor support (which is currently being provided by a number of donors and agencies).

People Movements and Cross-border Labor Markets

The ethnic groups in the wider Central Asia region for the most part spill across national boundaries. For example, most of Afghanistan's people have common ethnicity with groups in one or more neighboring countries. Ethnic Uzbeks are found in Tajikistan and Tajiks in Uzbekistan, and significant numbers of ethnic Russians are still found in former Soviet Central Asia, although many have emigrated to Russia in recent years. Its intermixed ethnic character (including numerous cases of cross-border family ties as well) is helping to bring the region closer together economically, but ethnic issues are also a source of political problems and disputes, both within and across countries.

Of particular economic importance and significant political sensitivity is labor migration from the poorer countries of the region in search of employment and income opportunities. The largest sending countries are Afghanistan, Tajikistan, and Uzbekistan, while Iran, Kazakhstan, Pakistan, and Russia are the major host countries for migrants from the region. During the long period of conflict, millions of Afghans took refuge in Pakistan and Iran. Some were in refugee camps but many others settled and found livelihoods. Although the majority of the estimated seven million Afghans in the two countries in 2001 have since returned to Afghanistan, several million remain. Similarly, during the period immediately following the dissolution of the Soviet Union, large-scale emigration occurred from Central Asia to Russia and Europe. These flows were "pushed" by crisis conditions in the sending countries.

More recently, the wider Central Asia region has seen the growth of economic migration across countries with different levels of development and diverging economic prospects, driven by both push and pull factors. Continuing outflows of labor from Afghanistan to Pakistan and Iran represent an important coping mechanism for the poor, often resorted to in the face of drought, other economic shocks, eradication of opium poppy crops, and so forth. These labor migrants are sending resources back home in the form or remittances or may personally return having acquired skills abroad. In post-Soviet Central Asia, millions of Tajiks, Kyrgyz, and Uzbeks are now temporary migrants in Kazakhstan and Russia, and remittances account for an estimated 20–30 percent of GDP in Tajikistan and 5–10 percent in the Kyrgyz Republic and Uzbekistan. Indeed, both Russia and Kazakhstan are considering policies to attract and formalize labor imports to balance an aging domestic population and support vibrant economic growth.

While economic migrants can provide significant benefits to the host countries, there are concerns in some countries, most notably Iran, related to competition for scarce jobs and fears that migrants are engaged in the narcotics trade.[6] Whereas Pakistan's labor market is relatively open to Afghans (for example, visas are granted freely), most of the countries in the wider Central Asia region restrict labor movements. Restrictions by recipient

---

6. Recent increases in wages in Afghanistan, driven by large inflows of donor funds and demand for construction services etc., have led to some reverse labor migration of skilled labor, however.

countries may hinder but do not stop labor flows; instead they drive such flows under-ground, which gives them considerable flexibility but with potentials for abuse, human trafficking, etc. Against this background, the major sending and host countries might con-sider concluding bilateral labor migration agreements, which would protect migrant work-ers, increase incentives to register in the host country, and thus allow more effective control over migrant populations and better protection of them from abuse and exploitation. Such an initiative is presently underway between Russia and Tajikistan but could be expanded to other countries across the region.

Short-term Recommendations

This cluster of issues is at the heart of the political constraints hindering regional economic cooperation, and progress particularly in addressing security and narcotics problems will take time. Nevertheless, there do appear to be some promising options for moving forward in the short run through relatively small steps, including the following:

- *Develop pilot schemes for cross border movement of goods and people within a limited border zone* to formalize existing informal movements.
- *Ensure adequate donor assistance to border guards* to fight against the drug trade, perhaps concentrated on a few pilot border posts along major trade and transit routes, to demonstrate how security concerns and trade facilitation can be simul-taneously addressed.
- *Develop bilateral agreements on temporary migration and greater data exchange and cooperation among border posts* (with the ultimate aim of shared border facilities).

Transport Infrastructure: Issues and Prospects

Much of the wider Central Asia region faces the predicament of being landlocked, result-ing in high transportation costs, reduced competition, and lower investment (Table 2.1). Numerous studies demonstrate that being landlocked has a negative impact on trade and economic growth.[7] Moreover, the negative effects of being landlocked are exacerbated by the number of borders that need to be crossed to reach major international seaports, as neighboring countries collect transit rents, and lack of harmonized trade and transit poli-cies raises trade costs.

Moreover, the geographical composition of intra-regional trade shows a notable bifurcation, with significant trade relations between Afghanistan, Iran, and Pakistan, some limited but growing trade between Iran and post-Soviet Central Asia, but virtually no trade between Pakistan, Afghanistan, and their northern neighbors (Appendix B). International transit trade through the region also is minimal, estimated at just $3.5 bil-lion in 2003 (ADB, 2005a).

Against this background, stabilization and reconstruction of Afghanistan represents an opportunity for Central Asian countries to diversify their international connections and

---

7. A description of various studies is presented in Raballand (2003).

Table 2.1. Comparative Costs of Shipping a Container from the USA to Selected CA Countries					
Country of Destination	City of Destination	Port of Entry	Cost in US$	Distance (in km)	Price per km (in US$)
Kazakhstan	Almaty	St. Petersburg	12000	10490	1.14
Kyrgyz Republic	Bishkek	St. Petersburg	12000	10478	1.15
Russia	Moscow	St. Petersburg	6000	7828	0.77
Turkey	Ankara	Izmir	4000	8733	0.46

Source: Stone (2001), p. 36–37.

to reduce the distance and the number of borders to be crossed to reach international maritime transportation hubs. For instance, the Central Asia–Afghanistan–Pakistan (Karachi port) road corridor would provide potentially one of the cheapest and probably quickest transit routes to and from Central Asia. The prospect of this route being reopened has already started to reshape the transportation landscape in the region by spurring competition over transit trade between Iran and Pakistan. Iran is currently undertaking some major investments in the construction of shorter road and railway links to the Iranian ports of Bandar Abbas and Chabahar, while Pakistan is seeking ways of linking its railways with those of Central Asian states. Figure 2.3 below summarizes the various land transportation

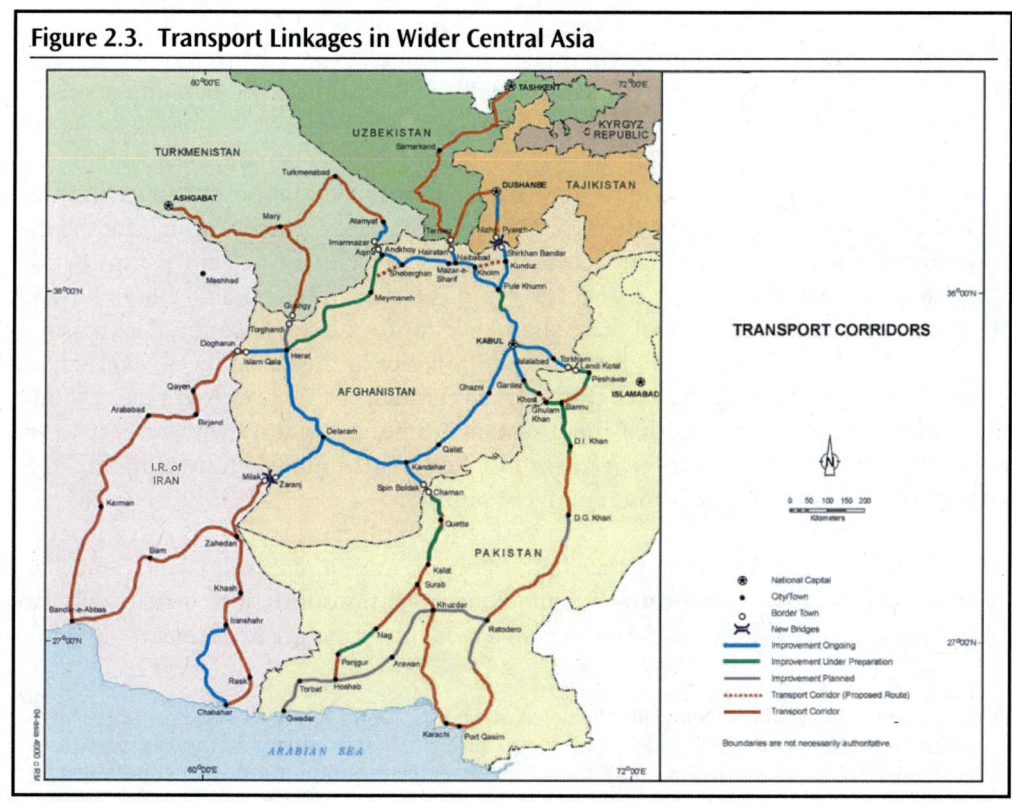

Figure 2.3. Transport Linkages in Wider Central Asia

Source: ADB (2005a).

routes currently under reconstruction or consideration. The Asian Development Bank has identified no less than 52 potential routes linking Central Asia with Iran and Pakistan. Since many of these routes require significant investments (rough estimates total over US$ 5 billion), there is clearly a need to prioritize, taking into account where the major bottlenecks are and where the benefits would be greatest (see Appendix B).

In addition there are transport connections between parts of the wider Central Asia region and neighboring countries outside the region, such as the dynamic economies of China and India as well as Russia and the Middle East, which offer both substantial markets and supply of goods. However, the internal barriers and obstacles within the region mean that these connections have not led to greater intra-regional integration so far. Moreover, in the case of India-Pakistan, improving transport connections, with positive implications for Central Asia and Afghanistan, depends on further progress in improving bilateral relations.

Little progress has occurred so far in the integration and reform of air transportation in the region. Given the significant security risks and costs of land transport, air transport could be a viable alternative for many goods, but this would necessitate greater competition and openness in the sector, as well as investments in airports and air traffic control (World Bank 2005b).

Improved transportation links would have important economic consequences for the region. Availability of a reliable and reasonably timely railway link out of Central Asia to compete with Russia's existing network would spur regional diversification of trade in the post-Soviet Central Asian republics. Faster road and air transportation could play a crucial role in diversification of the commodity composition of exports, increasing the region's competitiveness for time-sensitive goods, such as agroprocessing, industrial intermediates, and light consumer goods (Auty, Kunth, and Raballand 2005). Furthermore, the reconstruction of the road network in Afghanistan will facilitate other regional initiatives such as the construction of pipelines and electricity transmission lines.

Two caveats are in order, however. The extent to which planned trans-Afghanistan transport routes are used not just for trade from and with Central Asia but also for inter-regional transit trade depends on their competitiveness relative to existing links for the surrounding countries. Russia's main access to the Persian Gulf at present is through the Caspian and Iran, while China has direct access to Pakistan and the Indian Ocean through the Karakorum Highway. Both of these alternative routes face far fewer border crossings. There is certainly scope for additional competition, but in the face of these alternatives, demand forecasts for long-distance transit trade through the Central Asia region should be cautious. This also means that there remains some uncertainty with respect to the robustness of estimated economic returns of investments in major transport corridors. Getting these estimates right is thus an urgent priority.

Second, the economic returns to investments in physical transport infrastructure depend to a very large extent on parallel progress with trade and transit facilitation.[8] This, as well as the need to coordinate investments along major transportation corridors, dictates a carefully sequenced approach. Major regional road infrastructure investments, for exam-

---

8. Related to this point, it should also be noted that the economic return to transport infrastructure investments also depends on the quality of the infrastructure and the framework for financing maintenance. Hence such investments need to be accompanied by the development of institutions and mechanisms (including appropriate cost recovery) to ensure that quality standards are adequate and infrastructure is properly maintained.

ple, should follow improvements in trade facilitation and trade policies, rather than vice versa. An important implication of this point is that if one country steadfastly refuses to cooperate on trade and transit facilitation, second-best routes bypassing it might have to be developed. Another implication is that donors should look for "bold stroke" opportunities where selected investments may increase the returns to trade facilitation sufficiently to unlock progress on this front.[9] These approaches would benefit from a performance measurement system along different transport corridors to establish the extent and precise costs of policy procrastination.

Short-term Recommendations

The key to progress in the short run in this area will be ensuring that ongoing transport infrastructure investments are completed in a timely manner, remaining bottlenecks are addressed, and investments are well utilized and fully reap their envisaged benefits (requiring among other things trade and transit facilitation). Major new investments may require additional analytical work, in particular on the potential for transcontinental transit trade through the region, to determine priorities and the appropriate size of investments. Specific recommendations are as follows:

- *Undertake a review of all existing transportation routes to identify particular bottlenecks* and coordinate donor assistance for physical reconstruction to focus on such bottlenecks.
- *Carry out a complete review of interregional transit routes* by calculating current and anticipated future costs of inter-continental transit corridors through Central Asia (for example, Moscow-Delhi, Peking-Teheran, and so forth). Identify selected corridors that would allow cooperation on a pilot basis to demonstrate benefits quickly.
- *Develop carefully sequenced investments in the sector* to leverage improvements in bilateral or multilateral regulations affecting trade and transit. Opportunities for "bold strokes" may exist where investments in critical infrastructure could help unlock greater policy progress and coordination. Consider and develop cost estimates for routes bypassing countries unwilling to push forward the trade and transit facilitation agenda.
- *Progressively open up regional air transportation markets,* which would be expected to lead to a consolidation of the regional airline industry with potentially large economic benefits.

Prospects and Constraints for Development of Regional/Transit Trade

There are many obstacles to trade and transit within and across the region, which are summarized in Table 2.2. They are grouped here into obstacles related to trade policy, border

---

9. The bridge now being constructed across the Amu Darya between Tajikistan and Afghanistan may be an example of such a bold stroke. While initially the bridge is likely to be used only for local bilateral trade, it will open up a new transit route for Tajik goods to world markets, which avoids costly transit through Uzbekistan. This in turn may encourage Uzbekistan to reconsider its policies vis a vis Tajik transit trade.

Table 2.2. Major Trade and Transit Obstacles	
Trade Policy	• Differences in tariff rates • Different stages in the WTO accession process • Overlapping, sometimes inconsistent regional trade preferences • Non-tariff tax barriers such as excise taxes on imports, labeling requirements, import licenses
Border Management	• Lack of harmonized customs procedures, leading to detailed checks on both sides of the border • Numerous and cumbersome documentation requirements • Lack of recognition of TIR seals and high cost of transit convoys • Lengthy transshipment procedures and lack of adequate logistics (trade terminals, etc.) • High levels of corruption of customs officials and other inspection agencies
Transport Sector	• Visa restrictions on entry of foreign truckers • Truck entry fees • Trucking cartels to guarantee safe passage • Lack of modern (TIR compatible) trucking fleet • Slow speed of rail cargo leading to lack of competitiveness for time sensitive goods • Lack of freight forwarding companies that could offer smaller tonnage freights on rail cargo

management and customs harmonization, and regulation of the transportation sector, including in relation to competition and private sector investment.

From an economic perspective, reducing the costs of trade and transit would make sense under any circumstances, given that this has been identified as one of the main obstacles to the economic development of the region. Welfare improvements in the short run are likely to be largest for greater cooperation among neighboring countries, and between countries which already have significant trade flows. In the medium to long term, trade facilitation along transit corridors crossing several countries is likely to add significant benefits as well.

From the perspective of politicians, however, abolition of policy barriers often goes against powerful vested interests, whose rents may be at stake. Governments in the region therefore have sometimes tended to delay serious work on trade facilitation until the physical investments have been put in place, which would raise the returns to policy changes and thus potentially help build up greater political support to overcome opposing interests. The task for donors, therefore, is to identify those investment opportunities that would substantially increase the returns to policy change, and hold back investments where the prospect of leveraging policy changes is weak. Where political will to reform seems largely absent, the development of alternatives bypassing the countries with the most restrictive regimes should be costed and considered.

A first step to generate more political ownership for the trade facilitation agenda could be the creation of border stations and transit corridor performance measurement systems. The World Bank with the assistance of the private sector is developing such a system for nine corridors in Central Asia, and is working in a similar direction through customs projects in Afghanistan and Pakistan (for details see Appendix C). Exposing weaknesses and showing how small steps can lead to significant improvements has been a successful tool for engaging governments in regional cooperation in other parts of the world (for example, Southeastern Europe). In the short run, it may also be easier and highly beneficial to encourage greater cooperation at the national level between different border enforcement agencies, such as the customs, the road police, the security services, and so forth. Their lack of coordination can be as serious a factor in increasing the cost of cross-border movements of goods as lack of cooperation between countries. Afghanistan is a clear example of the need for such coordination; although the trade regime is open, the existence of numerous, uncoordinated, often illegal collections of fees and other taxes at the border and inside the country constitutes a nuisance to economic activity and deters firms from trading—especially in the formal sector.

For bilateral and multilateral cooperation between countries, using an external anchor, such as the WTO accession process, to guide harmonization efforts may provide additional impetus, although for several countries in the region WTO accession remains a distant prospect. For some countries at least (including Afghanistan, Tajikistan, and Uzbekistan) bilateral or regional agreements may offer good prospects for progress as long as these are consistent with subsequent multilateral liberalization and harmonization efforts. Any efforts at the regional level should facilitate and not hinder greater integration of the region in the global economy through multilateral agreements such as the WTO. Donor support to national customs or bilateral cooperation agreements should be designed in ways that fit into a wider regional and multilateral approach. Regional groups such as EurASEC and ShOS also may generate momentum for trade liberalization among a subset of countries, which could be expanded later. Particularly if these groups force highly protective countries to reduce their barriers, such forms of regionalism could be welfare enhancing overall.[10]

Some issues require more than just policy coordination in order to be resolved. For instance, existing entry barriers for trucks from neighboring countries are often justified based on concerns about their insufficient technical standards, and the lack of implementation of the TIR convention among post-Soviet states suffers in part from the same problem. One idea, proposed in this paper, is to create a specific donor-assisted regional transport fund, from which regional countries could draw subject to demonstrating action to reduce entry barriers for trucks that meet minimum standards. Similar links between infrastructure needs and the ability to effectively deal with policy barriers exist in border management, where donor investments in upgrading border posts could be made contingent on greater bilateral willingness to share information and harmonize procedures across border posts.

It should be noted that even small improvements in trade facilitation could have a significant impact on people's livelihoods, if they facilitate informal trade and encourage it to become formal. Security improvements in Afghanistan are likely to be the key for the promotion of this kind of trade, creating employment for both Afghans and other Central Asians. Overcoming and managing concerns about potential spill-over of security problems from Afghanistan into other Central Asian countries, and also among the post-Soviet Central Asian countries, will be critical in this regard. As argued in Appendix C, this requires positive incentives more than tighter controls. One specific proposal in this regard

---

10. While there is an important debate on the trade diversion effects of regional trade blocks, given the high levels of mutual trade dependency, for instance among the EurASEC members, reducing barriers to trade among them in the context of a regional agreement is likely to be welfare enhancing. EurASEC foresees initially a Free Trade Agreement to be later expanded into a customs union. The latter is likely to happen after Russia has joined the WTO, and its external tariff has thus been set.

is the creation of border zones within which informal traders (and perhaps even formal trade) can enter the more protected markets in the region against a fee, set well below the current rates of protection. In this way, informal trade would have an incentive to become formal, employment opportunities would be created on both sides of the border, the host country (the protected market) would collect more customs revenues and capture some of the arbitrage rents from informal traders, while—by restricting the arrangement to a specific border zone—security concerns could be more easily managed. It is interesting that in the border town of Kara-Su between Uzbekistan and the Kyrgyz Republic, where a large bazaar has sprung up on the Kyrgyz side to supply informal traders bringing goods into Uzbekistan, the Uzbek authorities recently opened a free border crossing point and are considering the construction of a bazaar on their side of the border. Pakistan has a long tradition of similar, less publicly regulated, bazaars for goods imported unofficially through Afghanistan for sale on the domestic market.

Short-term Recommendations

A combination of regulatory improvements, easing burdens on the private sector, capacity building, and relatively small investments will yield high dividends in this area. As the changes required will affect different interest groups inside and outside the governments of the countries concerned, progress will require political will and may be uneven across countries. Specific recommendations for the short run include the following:

- *Create a performance measurement system for border stations and transit corridors,* so that progress in improving their performance can be transparently assessed, with feedback about problems so that they can be addressed.
- *Harmonize primary legislation for customs as well as documentation requirements* in each country in line with Kyoto Convention and the WTO.
- *Improve coordination between border enforcement agencies at the national level,* for example, through the creation of a National Trade Facilitation Council.
- *Increase bilateral border management cooperation,* such as data exchanges, mutual recognition of customs documentation, and so forth.[11] Donor support to customs and other border institutions should be designed in ways that leverage such cooperation but ensure that any bilateral agreements allow for easy extension to other countries.
- *Develop cross-border zones that offer visa free movement for informal traders,* and establish special border markets where informal traders can sell and buy goods for a fee that is discounted from existing tariff and excise rates.
- *Consider the establishment of a truck modernization fund with donor assistance,* which would help upgrade national fleets to meet minimum performance standards, subject to concrete measures by regional countries to reduce entry barriers for trucks from neighboring countries, such as truck entry bans or fees, convoy requirements for transit trucks even under TIR, and cumbersome visa requirements for truckers.

---

11. Several such bilateral agreements have already been concluded. See Report of the Transport and Trade Facilitation Committee to CAREC, October 2005, and Appendix C for details.

Additional proposals, which may require more time, include:

- ▓ *Enforce the TIR convention among post-Soviet countries* and consider the establishment of a temporary alternative transit insurance system for wider Central Asia.
- ▓ *Create one common visa zone for all post-Soviet Central Asian countries* (for instance in the context of EurASEC), and reduce visa fees for non-CIS members
- ▓ *Create a regional association of transport operators* to lobby for improved regulation and enforce a self-policing regime.

Energy Development and Energy Trade Prospects

Potential

The wider Central Asia region has substantial energy resources, and there is variation across countries in the amounts and types of energy endowments (see Table 2.3). Whereas Iran and UAE have large oil reserves and—together with nearby Qatar, Russia, Turkmenistan, Pakistan and to a lesser extent certain other countries—sizable natural gas reserves, the

Table 2.3. Primary Energy Resources in Wider Central Asia (WCA) and Main Neighbors

Type of Reserves	Crude Oil	Natural Gas	Coal	Total**		Hydro Potential	
Countries\Units	MTOE*	MTOE	MTOE	MTOE	% of Total	TWh/year	% of Total
Afghanistan	–	–	–	–	–	–	–
Kazakhstan	5404	2700	19810	27914	77%	62	12%
Kyrgyz Republic	6	5	580	591	2%	99	19%
Tajikistan	2	5	500	507	1%	317	62%
Turkmenistan	74	2610	Insignificant	2684	7%	5	1%
Uzbekistan	81	1674	2851	4606	13%	27	5%
Subtotal Central Asian countries:	5567	6994	23741	36302	100%	510	100%
Iran	18068	24750	–	42818	21%	88	4%
Pakistan	–	718	1017	1735	1%	130	5%
Russia	9859	43200	68699	121758	60%	1670	70%
Subtotal WCA:	33494	75662	93457	202613	100%	2398	100%
China	2328	2006	58900	63,234	18%	1920	37%
India	759	831	60843	62,433	18%	660	13%
Turkey	–	–	1488	1,488	0%	216	4%
UAE	13340	5454	–	18,794	5%	–	–
Total for WCA plus main neighbors:	49921	83953	214688	348562	100%	5194	100%

*Million Tons of Oil Equivalents.
**Does not include hydropower generation potential.
Source: World Bank (2004).

mountainous countries of Tajikistan, the Kyrgyz Republic, and Afghanistan have considerable hydropower potential, much of it undeveloped. The larger countries in and around the region, particularly in South Asia, comprise major sources of demand for energy, much of which cannot be satisfied from domestic sources. Although energy demand from Afghanistan is limited by, most notably, the extremely limited coverage of population through its small electricity grids, there are significant gaps between existing demand and supply, the filling of which is considered of high priority for Afghanistan's reconstruction agenda in the short run.

Thus there is prima facie great potential for regional energy development and trade which can benefit all of the countries of the region. More specifically, there would appear to be good prospects for development of hydel resources in the countries with large potential (Tajikistan and over time the Kyrgyz Republic and Afghanistan), much of whose output could be exported to electricity-deficit countries to the North (Russia) or South (notably Pakistan) as well as to Iran in the West. Similarly, there are opportunities for natural gas trade from gas-surplus countries like Turkmenistan and Iran to gas-deficit countries like Pakistan and India.

Constraints

There are also important constraints and impediments to coordinated development and trade of energy resources in the wider Central Asia region:

- *Security:* In particular Afghanistan, but also some of the other countries of the region, suffer from insecurity in certain geographical areas, which could adversely affect the construction and operation of infrastructure for energy trade (such as transmission lines and natural gas pipelines).
- *Energy security:* Some countries may be concerned about dependence on energy imports, of electricity in particular, from other countries. This may reflect past conflicts and disputes, or concerns about the political stability of energy exporters and transmission routes and the ability to honor long-term export commitments. On the other hand, energy exporting countries may be concerned about payment arrangements and reliability and stability of demand.
- *Political competition over transmission routes:* Energy transmission networks often have "network monopoly" characteristics, which means that in many cases there are discrete either-or choices about transmission routes. Such choices easily can become the subject of destructive geopolitical competition, with the risk of technically and financially attractive routes being blocked and possibly inferior routes chosen due to geopolitical factors. A good example is the competition between alternative routes for a gas pipeline from Turkmenistan to Pakistan (see Box 2.1).
- *Infrastructure:* There is a lack of transregional energy infrastructure (electricity transmission lines and gas pipelines), and the national energy networks in a number of the countries are limited, most notably in Afghanistan, which affects the ability to transfer and utilize energy. Major investments in electricity generation and gas production capacity also would be required to exploit regional potentials.
- *Institutions:* The regulatory framework for regional energy planning, investment financing, investment protection, contract enforcement, and policy and commercial risk mitigation is weak, and there are major institutional weaknesses in many of the regional countries.

Box 2.1. Turkmenistan–Pakistan–India Gas Pipeline

The possibility of a pipeline to transfer natural gas from Turkmenistan through Afghanistan to Pakistan, and perhaps from there onward to India, has been under discussion for more than a decade. Such a pipeline would diversify export options for Turkmenistan, supply energy-short Pakistan and India, and provide Afghanistan with transit fees as well as enhanced access to natural gas. However, the proposal gives rise to issues related to security in Afghanistan, uncertainty about gas reserves in Turkmenistan, strained production capacities there, and a competing Iran-Pakistan-India gas pipeline project. The prospects for Pakistan-India gas trade are further complicated by political factors.

Thus the issue of a gas pipeline from Turkmenistan to Pakistan and India is a matter of competition between Iran and Afghanistan, and subject to larger geopolitical issues. Partly to increase the prospects for the Iran route to be implemented, Iran has recently financed a pipeline that runs from Korpedzh in Turkmenistan to Kurt Kui in northern Iran, and has started importing gas from Turkmenistan. The United States supports construction of the trans-Afghanistan pipeline, in part because the associated transit fees are seen as an important long-term source of income for Afghanistan, and in part because it opposes the alternative trans-Iran project. Russia's Gazprom, on the other hand, opposes the trans-Afghanistan line as it wants to maintain a monopoly over the transport of Central Asian gas and utilize that gas as a relatively cheap source of incremental supply for domestic markets and re-export. Partly to further this goal, Gazprom supports the trans-Iran project.

In early September, Pakistan and India agreed to finalize by the end of 2005 a framework agreement for construction of the gas pipeline from Iran, which may begin in the middle of 2007 (pending third-party certification of Iran's gas reserves) and could be finished by 2010.

In spite of these difficult issues, there may be possibilities to explore mutually beneficial options if the different stakeholders are willing. One example is the possibility that a gas pipeline from Iran to Pakistan might enable supply of gas to nearby parts of Afghanistan.

- *Energy sector policies:* The countries in the region have differing energy pricing policies and other policies (e.g., toward private sector participation) which may constrain energy trade, or allow it to occur on an uneconomic basis. Combined with weak institutions, this further increases risks and reduces rates of return on potential investments.
- *Water issues:* In the case of hydropower, which potentially can serve as the production base for substantial regional electricity trade, there are in many cases riparian issues which would need to be resolved for major investments to go ahead.

Short-term Recommendations

Given the promising activities already underway in the electricity sector, the great potential for energy development in the region over the medium term, and the complementarities among regional countries in terms of resources and demand, this is a priority area for concrete progress and results in the short run. The suggested approach is to use power exports to Afghanistan along existing transmission lines or new relatively lower-capacity lines to meet the country's internal needs and build confidence and leverage institutional changes (such as the signing of power trading agreements and domestic energy price reform where needed). This will set a foundation for larger-scale electricity trade based on substantial investments, and over the longer-term for integration of electricity markets.

There is also scope for subgroups of regional countries to pursue major investments in electricity development and trade in their mutual interest, for example export of hydropower from Tajikistan to/through Afghanistan to Pakistan. As suggested earlier, electricity trade would be a good entry point for subsequent cooperation on water issues, starting from the perspective of hydropower. Key recommendations for the short run are as follows:

- *Formalize power trading agreements* between Afghanistan and neighbors where appropriate (that is, there is mutual agreement for stable multi-year trade), in order to regularize bilateral electricity trade. Such agreements, which need to include payment arrangements that provide confidence to the electricity exporting countries, would lay the foundation for longer-term exchange. Donor technical assistance for designing agreements should be provided as needed.
- *Accelerate construction of critical transmission infrastructure* in order to ensure that this does not become a bottleneck to expanding electricity trade.
- *Conduct a study on regional energy markets* that includes all countries in the wider Central Asia region, building on the Regional Energy Export Potential Study for post-Soviet Central Asia, and fully in line with the analytical work envisaged by ECO.
- *Solicit private sector interest* in longer-term investments in generation and transmission systems, focusing first on run-of the river hydel opportunities (which do not raise riparian issues) and thermal generation.
- *Continue the development of an institutional framework* within which longer-term issues of energy development and trade, and possible integration of electricity markets, can be discussed and resolved. This could involve extending membership of the Energy Charter Conference, which provides a framework for electricity trade in a growing Eurasian market, to Afghanistan and also the SAARC countries. Central Asian states are already members, and China and Iran are observers. Afghanistan has indicated that it will consider joining the Energy Charter Conference. ECO also is providing a useful forum for the wider Central Asia region to share information, discuss regional energy issues, and provide an umbrella for regional energy studies.

Water Development, Use, and Management

Water is the scarce natural resource in most of the wider Central Asia region. Moreover, there are very important riparian relationships between many regional countries, not all of them covered by water-sharing agreements. Afghanistan utilizes only a small proportion (estimated roughly at around 30 percent) of the water resources that originate in the country, and water would inevitably comprise an important component of its longer-term development strategy. At the same time, other countries in the region depend to a greater or lesser extent on waters flowing from Afghanistan and obviously have a stake in future water utilization. There is major scope for more efficient utilization of water in all of the countries in the region. As emphasized earlier in this chapter, water issues are potentially closely interlinked with other major regional issues like narcotics and people movements, as well as (on account of hydropower) energy development and trade. Thus, from a medium-term perspective, water will be a very important component of regional economic cooperation and development prospects.

It makes sense to look at water issues from a river basin perspective. The discussion below briefly reviews some of the main river basins in the wider Central Asia region.

Amu Darya River

The Amu Darya River is the largest river in Central Asia and the second largest river in Afghanistan in terms of total flow. The total irrigated area served by the Amu Darya is about 6 million ha (distributed among countries as shown in Table 2.4), and much economic activity is located in the Amu Darya basin. The river is the major contributor to the dying Aral Sea. The main upstream riparian countries are Afghanistan and Tajikistan, while the main downstream riparian countries are Turkmenistan and Uzbekistan.

According to Ahmad and Wasiq (2004), the only existing agreement on Amu Darya water sharing is that of 1987. This agreement reflected the internal central administrative decision of the Soviet Union and set maximum water distribution limits for Central Asian countries (Table 2.4). Afghanistan was not part of this agreement; however, usage of 2.1 billion cubic meters (bcm) per year on the part of Afghanistan was assumed. A recent document prepared by the Government of Afghanistan suggests that under an older, 1946 agreement, Afghanistan could use up to 9 bcm (or 15 percent) of the Amu Darya flow annually. Afghanistan has never actually utilized such a large amount of water from the Amu Darya. Due to the deterioration of irrigation systems during the conflict, without significant new investments it is estimated that it would take Afghanistan about a decade to reach the 1990 level of its Amu Darya water consumption of 5 bcm annually. For the sake of comparison, it should be noted that Turkmenistan and Uzbekistan could easily reduce their water consumption by some 8 bcm per year by improving their water management practices. Therefore, increased utilization of Amu Darya water resources by Afghanistan is unlikely to become a serious issue for the other riparian countries in the immediate future. However, over the medium term major irrigation investments clearly will be required for Afghanistan's agricultural development and also to provide employment and alternative

Table 2.4. Irrigated Land in the Amu Darya Basin					
	Average Annual Flow by Riparian Country (bcm/year)	**% of Total Flow**	**Irrigated Area in Amu Darya Basin (million ha)**	**Maximum Distribution Limits* (bcm/year)**	**% of Total Limits**
Tajikistan	49.6	66	0.5	9.5	15.4
Afghanistan	17	23	1.16	–	–
Uzbekistan	5.1	7	2.3	29.9	48.2
Kyrgyz Republic	1.6	2	0.1	0.4	0.6
Turkmenistan	1.5	2	1.7	22	35.8
Total:	74.8	100	5.76	61.5	100

Notes: The distribution limits reflect the 1987 Soviet imposed agreement for the Central Asian republics. Afghanistan was not part of the agreement at that time.
bcm = billion cubic meters.
Source: Ahmad and Wasiq (2004).

livelihoods as part of the counternarcotics strategy. Thus Afghanistan has indicated its willingness to engage in serious discussions with its northern neighbors on utilization of water from the Amu Darya.[12]

Helmand River

Implementation of the existing Helmand River agreement between Iran and Afghanistan is a significant regional water management issue. The Helmand River originates in Afghanistan and is shared by Afghanistan and Iran primarily. The river used to provide an average of 4 bcm of water annually, but in the late 1990s, mainly because of the drought in Afghanistan, its annual volume fell to 0.3 bcm, greatly reducing the flow of water to Hamon Lake in Iran. This dried up the lake, causing serious economic losses and environmental damage. On the other hand, Afghanistan's major water storage facility on the Helmand River, the Kajakai Dam and associated lake, have suffered from destruction and lack of maintenance during the long period of conflict, and much of the irrigation system is only partly functional. Thus rehabilitation of this system is of high priority for Afghanistan. Over the longer term, Afghanistan would most probably expect to make new water conservancy investments in the Helmand basin. The situation with implementation of the Helmand agreement has reportedly improved since 2002 with the easing of the drought in Afghanistan, but both sides seem to be still not fully satisfied with its substance/implementation. The last talks between Iran and Afghanistan on this matter took place in the fall 2004 and were inconclusive.

Kabul River

This is the main river basin in southeastern Afghanistan, and the Kabul River is a major tributary of the Indus River which it joins at Attock in Pakistan. There has never been an international agreement on the division of flow from the Kabul River. It is estimated that Afghanistan utilizes only 10 percent of the Kabul River flow and that 90 percent is utilized by Pakistan. There are some modest pre-war water conservancy systems and hydroelectric facilities along the Kabul River in Afghanistan, which deteriorated during the conflict and are in urgent need of rehabilitation. On the other hand, Pakistan has made major investments in water conservancy and hydropower along the Indus River, both above and below where it is joined by the Kabul River. In the absence of an international agreement, it appears that neither country has consulted with the other in the past about these investments, which particularly in the case of the Indus have had potentially major impacts on the use of Kabul River water.

It is apparent even from this abbreviated summary discussion that water issues in the wider Central Asia region, particularly those related to Afghanistan but also some involving other countries in the region, are contentious. The importance of water for the region

---

12. A proposal has recently been developed for a major new dam at Dashtijum on the Afghan-Tajik border along the Pandzh river (a major tributary to the Amu Darya). Size (4,000 MW) and estimated cost (several US$ billions) are very large, and there are potentially major implications in terms of the resulting control over the river flow by upstream countries for downstream riparians. Even if the economic benefits can be established, this project idea exemplifies the political challenges of water allocation issues.

as a whole and for the individual countries means that it cannot be ignored, and that progress will yield high rewards. One question is whether the time is ripe for countries concerned to discuss and possibly reach agreement on water sharing, perhaps in the context of a coordinated set of investments in both upstream and downstream riparian countries. The readiness for this type of initiative may vary across the different river basins.

Short-term Recommendations

Although there may not be prospects for dramatic progress of a "breakthrough" nature on water issues in the near future, it is extremely important that processes of information collection, consultation, and participation be initiated, to provide a sound foundation that will pave the way for broader agreements later on water sharing and improved water utilization in the region.

- *Concerted efforts to measure water flows and use in Afghanistan,* for which the information base is very weak.
- *Accelerated rehabilitation of existing water conservancy facilities in Afghanistan,* which does not raise riparian issues.
- *Participation by Afghanistan in existing riparian groups,* specifically for the Amu Darya; this could initially be on a special basis if there is no existing agreement including Afghanistan.
- *Initiation/continuation of technical-level dialogue* between Iran and Afghanistan with respect to the Helmand River and between Pakistan and Afghanistan with respect to the Kabul River. It was agreed at the Kabul Conference on Regional Economic Cooperation to set up working groups consisting of the concerned riparian countries for the Amu Darya, Kabul, and Helmand rivers, which marks a significant step forward.
- *Further technical work and consolidation of existing work on improving water utilization,* which can benefit all countries in the region.

CHAPTER 3

Entry Points and Ways Forward

Framework and Approach

The analysis in this paper has developed a framework for approaching regional cooperation in the wider Central Asia region. The framework is based on two fundamental analytical findings:

- *Critical linkages among sectors:* The following have been identified: (i) between border management, security, narcotics, labor movements, and trade and transit facilitation; (ii) between transport infrastructure and trade and transport facilitation; (iii) between narcotics production and trafficking, irrigation investments and water allocation along the major river basins, and cross-border labor movements; and (iv) between electricity trade, hydropower generation, and water issues. The paper argues that awareness of these linkages, and of how some sectors may be able to serve as entry points for tackling other, more difficult sectors, is essential for achieving real progress in regional economic cooperation.
- *Political obstacles to progress and corresponding need for political incentives:* The track record on regional cooperation has been modest to date. This is a reflection of the strength of the obstacles—in part physical and financial but to a large extent political—that are blocking progress. Rather than frontal attacks on political obstacles that may have little chance of success in the short run, the paper suggests a two-pronged approach: (i) in the short-term the focus should be on "win-win" initiatives that aim to build mutual confidence and ease political concerns; and (ii) these initiatives should be complemented by a few selected "bold strokes" where donor support could help increase and alter the distribution of benefits from regional cooperation in ways that make a visible breakthrough possible. Both

approaches are expected to build the basis for more far-reaching and institutionalized regional cooperation and associated domestic reforms in the future.

To move forward with this agenda, the paper advocates that governments and partners in
the region should, first, keep the "big picture" issues of regional cooperation and development in mind, even if immediate prospects for progress in some areas are limited, and also
clearly recognize and acknowledge the important linkages among sectors and the nature
of the obstacles faced. Second, governments and partners should identify and mutually
agree on areas where there are good possibilities for near-term success (based on mutually
beneficial, less controversial projects) and which may serve as entry points for further
progress including in other, more difficult sectors. Third, prioritized, intensive work
(including further analysis to robustly establish estimated benefits) is needed on these few
selected areas, with regular monitoring of progress and feedback to decisionmakers so that
improvements can be made as needed, as well as further steps forward made as possible.
Some of the existing regional organizations, if revitalized, may be able to play such a monitoring and feedback role. Fourth, capacity building will be essential, most notably in the
case of Afghanistan but also in some of the other regional countries and in some of the
regional organizations, if they have potential to play an important role in fostering regional
economic cooperation.

Finally, it must be recognized that, given the differences in economic policy regimes
and other differences outlined in Chapter 1, opportunities for progress are unlikely to be
spread evenly throughout the region but will often involve subgroups of countries and
sometimes bilateral cooperation between different pairings of countries. Such opportunities should be exploited and may themselves encourage similar initiatives involving other
regional countries. Examples include electricity trade (notably small-scale imports of
power into Afghanistan from different neighboring countries, as well as larger electricity
trading initiatives that are financially and economically attractive), creation of cross-border
zones with visa-free movement for informal traders, and dialogue on water issues, among
others. However, in some areas—such as harmonization of customs procedures, visa policies, border management initiatives, transit standards, and so forth—there are important
advantages to coordinated regional initiatives, so these should be pursued as is already
occurring in some cases.

Ways Forward in Three Areas

The Appendixes of this paper focus on three areas where, in the light of the analysis of the
main issues affecting regional cooperation, prospects for progress in the short run were
deemed to be good: cooperation in the electricity sector (Appendix A), regional transportation links (Appendix B), and trade and transit facilitation (Appendix C).

As the detailed discussion in the three Appendixes explains, perhaps the greatest
prospects for quick win-win initiatives at the regional level are in *electricity trade*.
Afghanistan's power needs, and the willingness of donors to fund investments in building
transmission infrastructure, create relatively low-risk export opportunities for countries
such as Tajikistan, Turkmenistan, and Uzbekistan. Pakistan may also supply some neighboring provinces of Afghanistan in the short run, and Iran is already doing so. Successful

exploitation of such opportunities for bilateral trade in electricity will build a track record of cooperation and momentum for larger-scale initiatives. There are also possibilities for one or more "bold stroke" projects with large benefits for a number of regional countries and significant private sector participation; although such projects will take time to implement, initial discussions are already occurring in some cases (e.g. investments in Tajikistan's hydel potential and associated power exports from Tajikistan to Pakistan). On the basis of progress with these initiatives, prospects may open up over the medium term for developing a regional power market, with major electricity flows and benefits, and correspondingly requiring much larger investments.

In *trade and transport,* the potential gains from regional cooperation are large, but unequally distributed both within and between countries. Hence quick-win solutions will require a greater degree of political buy-in and leadership from the governments in the region, as well as selectivity and focus by donors in order to leverage their financial support. Perhaps the best chance for achieving multilateral progress lies in establishing performance benchmarks to highlight the urgency and the benefits of action. It may also be possible to identify particular transport corridors where the benefits of cooperation could be clearly demonstrated. Donors should structure their assistance in a way that maximizes these opportunities. In the meantime, national trade facilitation policies and bilateral agreements should be designed in ways that would fit easily into a wider regional approach. External anchors such as the WTO accession process or the different existing regional cooperation organizations could be used to help coordinate national policies. Investments to rehabilitate transport corridors need to be sequenced in ways that are coordinated among different donors along major routes, and recognize and reward countries for demonstrated progress in trade facilitation. As a way of generating additional pressure, transport routes bypassing countries dragging their feet on trade facilitation and economic cooperation should be costed and may be considered for donor funding.

With respect to *trade facilitation,* the liberalization of trade policies—in the protected markets of Uzbekistan and Turkmenistan and in the liberalizing but still protected markets of Pakistan and Iran—is politically sensitive, and on a region-wide basis it most likely will be a longer-term endeavor. However, individual countries in the region which have liberalized their trade regimes and those which are currently doing so are encouraged to continue and deepen the trade liberalization process. As this paper has argued, current trade policies and restrictions do not effectively protect the domestic markets of countries with restrictive trade regimes but simply push trade and people movements into the informal sector. The paper therefore suggests as a short-term measure the creation of cross-border zones for countries with more restrictive trade regimes, where goods and people can move more freely. This would generate new employment opportunities for the poor in border areas, and would also help separate out informal trade in goods from narcotics and crime by creating incentives for informal traders to declare their products. If limited to individuals, such a relaxation would not pose a major competitive threat to domestic producers in the protected markets. More formalized arrangements may also be conceivable. This proposal would enable border guards and customs officials to concentrate on stopping criminals and controlling large cargo, rather than dissipating efforts and resources interacting with small individual traders—particularly since such interactions often serve as a vehicle for corruption.

The paper also offers some short-term recommendations for initiatives relating to *labor movements and water issues,* but the resolution of larger regional issues in both areas is likely to be politically sensitive and difficult, and will probably take more time. Nevertheless, the proposed initiatives will help pave the way for further progress when that becomes possible. The agreement at the Kabul Conference to set up multi-country working groups for the Amu Darya, Kabul, and Helmand river basins is a significant positive step in this regard.

Concluding Comments

Governments of the countries of the wider Central Asia region may be encouraged to cooperate with each other in the awareness of the important linkages between sectors, of the political constraints that they are facing themselves, and therefore of the need for careful sequencing of measures to achieve maximum impact and progress over time. Acknowledging openly what will be politically possible and what is unlikely to be possible in the short run would be a first confidence-building measure. Where certain countries are demonstrating unwillingness to engage in regional cooperation in important areas of mutual benefit, the other countries who are interested in moving forward may start exploring second-best solutions, bypassing countries that refuse to enter into a substantive dialogue on regional cooperation. Such solutions ultimately would attract donor funding. It is hoped that all regional countries will recognize the benefits of greater regional cooperation and—through short-term measures along the lines suggested—progressively build the trust and momentum that will make such bypass solutions unnecessary.

This paper has focused on initiatives that governments of regional countries could take to find ways forward in regional economic cooperation (individually, in subgroups, or at the wider regional level). However, the roles of other stakeholders in enhancing regional economic cooperation also are extremely important and must be recognized. Nearby as well as more distant countries (including the G-8 members that participated in the Kabul Conference) can play a very important supporting and enabling role. The private sector is a potent force for change and has a strong interest in the regional economic cooperation agenda.[13] The informal part of the private sector can be a source of entrepreneurship, dynamism, and formal sector development if the business climate is improved. The potential importance of regional organizations has been emphasized earlier in this paper. Multilateral institutions also have been working to help advance the regional development and economic cooperation agenda, and stand ready to continue to do so. And civil society, including the media, can play an important positive role.

Finally, it should be emphasized that the analysis and proposals in this paper are preliminary and are intended to generate further discussion and consideration. Above all, these issues, and the proposals for entry points and ways forward, need to be carefully considered by the regional countries themselves. The concrete ideas are perhaps less important than the analytical framework and overall approach put forward in the paper.

---

13. While there may be opposition from some private sector interest groups to certain policy changes, for example trade liberalization or opening up the trucking sector in countries hitherto characterized by restrictive policies, private sector associations can be developed and can play an advocacy role for targeted improvements.

APPENDIXES

Prospects for Electricity Trade

As discussed in Chapter 2 of this paper, the wider Central Asia region has considerable potential for development of energy resources as well as expanding energy trade, but there are major constraints that need to be addressed in order for this potential to be realized. However, some regional electricity trade based on existing power surpluses and gaps is already occurring, including relatively modest electricity imports by Afghanistan from neighboring countries to make up for extremely limited domestic generation capacity and fragmented local grid systems. If managed properly, further development of this trade represents a good short-run option for moving forward, building confidence and a track record of regional cooperation (on a bilateral basis initially, but increasingly multilateral over time), and setting a good foundation for major exploitation of energy development and trade potentials. Electricity trade may also provide a good entry point for making progress over time on water issues, first from the hydropower perspective and then on the more difficult water issues associated with irrigation use.

The sequence of actions would thus be first to regularize and expand ongoing electricity trade and prioritize ongoing efforts to achieve quick "wins" like the transmission line from northern Afghanistan to Kabul and associated imports of electricity from Uzbekistan as well as possible imports from Tajikistan. Options for further development of electricity trade should be exploited, and possible "breakthrough" projects involving significant investments and substantial electricity trading opportunities could be explored, particularly with private sector participation. Progress in these areas would set the stage for more systematic exploitation of the large potential for electricity trade over the medium term, which would need to start with a fully region-wide study of electricity potential and trade, building on the existing and planned analytical work at subregional and country levels.

This Appendix first looks at the current patterns of electricity trade in the region and in particular for Afghanistan, and discusses near-term options for accelerating progress.

The first section of this Appendix concludes with a brief discussion of options for more sizable "breakthrough" projects which could be considered. The second section summarizes medium-term prospects for electricity development and trade in the region and possibilities for electricity exports to surrounding countries. The third section recommends some ways forward to realize the potential for regional electricity trade.

Current Patterns of Electricity Trade and Near-Term Options

Current Electricity Production and Trade

As can be seen from Table A.1, some countries in the region are large producers of electricity, and some of them export or import substantial amounts of power. In particular, all of the immediate neighboring countries, with the exception of Pakistan, export small amounts of electricity to Afghanistan. This trade occurs on an ad hoc basis without contractual agreements (power purchase agreements, PPAs). Though the amounts are relatively small, this trade represents an opportunity to achieve modest yet significant mutually beneficial results in the short run, and there is potential for expansion, discussed later in this Appendix.

There is in addition to the Afghan electricity imports more substantial trade occurring between other Central Asian countries and also with Russia. Table A.2 presents an electricity trade matrix for the countries in the wider Central Asia region and some other nearby countries. In the case of Iran, in addition to the interconnection with Afghanistan, trading takes place with Armenia, Azerbaijan, Pakistan, Turkey, and Turkmenistan, with Iran importing about 1.5 Twh per year. New transmission lines are under construction for increased trade with Turkmenistan, which is expected to increase imports from Turkmenistan alone to 2.4 Twh per year. The existing trade and near-term plans demonstrate that there is indeed good potential for the future.

Afghanistan's Current Situation

Afghanistan has considerable energy resources, but there is uncertainty about their quantities. The country's fossil fuel resources are thought to comprise some 30 billion cubic meters of proven gas reserves,[14] 95 million barrels of oil and condensate reserves; and coal reserves in excess of 100 million tons. However, engineering, costing, and market analysis work is needed to improve on these outdated reserve estimates and evaluate how much can be commercially exploited. Afghanistan also has a considerable amount of hydroelectric potential. On account of the prolonged conflict, the energy infrastructure of Afghanistan could not grow beyond the level reached in the mid-1970s and in fact considerably deteriorated on account of war damage and lack of maintenance. As of 2003, the country's installed electricity generation capacity was reported to be 454 MW, with operable capacity believed to be only 285 MW.

Demand has been rising but is still below 1.0 TWh, and the present peak load is assumed to be 215 MW for all of Afghanistan. There is also probably a suppressed demand, which is assumed to be 0.5 TWh in energy terms and 120 MW in peak power needs.

---

14. Total natural gas reserves, including unproven reserves, may be 2–3 times this amount.

Table A.1. Electricity Production and Trade by Selected Regional Countries

Afghanistan	Iran	Kazakhstan	Pakistan	Tajikistan	Turkmenistan	Uzbekistan
In 2003/04: - produced: 0.645 TWh - consumed: 0.855 TWh - imported: 0.255 TWh - exported: 0.0 TWh Net Importer. Only an estimated 10% of the population has access to electricity through grids.	In 2003: prod: 149 TWh cons: 150 TWh imp: 1.9 TWh exp: 0.9 TWh Iran supplies electricity to Afghanistan, in some areas directly adjacent to the Afghan-Iranian border in Herat, Farah, and Nimroz provinces. Reportedly, Iran plans to increase power supplies to Afghanistan's Herat province from Khorasan.	In 2004 prod: 67 TWh cons: 64.8 TWh imp: 5.2 TWh exp: 7.4 TWh Imports from: Russia, 2.3 TWh; Kyrgyz Rep., 2.9 TWh; Tajik, 0.8 GWh. Exports to Russia: 7.4 TWh	In 2003: prod: 75.3 TWh cons: 52.7 TWh imp: 0 TWh exp: 0 TWh Currently Pakistan is self-sufficient in electricity. Substantial system losses (including theft) eat up the surplus power generated. Yet since the year 2000 the country has been experiencing rapid economic growth and is turning net electric power importer.	In 2004 (source: WB): Prod: 16,3 TWh Cons: 16,4 TWh Total imports: 4,7 TWh Total exports: 4,6 TWh Import from Uzbekistan 4.7 TWh; export to Uzbekistan 4.1 TWh; export to Kyrgyzstan 0.2 TWh; export to Afghanistan 0.028 TWh. Exports to Russia: 0.2 TWh in 2003 but 0 in 2004. Currently it is net albeit seasonal importer but has some seasonal surplus capacity for hydropower exports to Uzbekistan, Kazakhstan and especially to Afghanistan, Iran and Pakistan. Currently it has about 1.6–2.7 TWh excess/exportable capacity. Yet its hydroelectric potential 40 GW with an energy content of about 317–527 TWh annually of which only 5–10% has so far been developed. In May of 2003 Tajikistan resumed supply to Kunduz province in northern Afghanistan, although supplies were expected to halt in October of 2003.	prod: 11.4 TWh (2004) cons: 8.9 TWh (2002) imp: 0 TWh (2002) exp: 1.1 TWh (2004) Net exporter. Turkmenistan supplies electricity to much of northern area including Mazar-i-Sharif and Heart. The arrangement was affirmed in an agreement between Karzai government and Turkmenistan in April of 2002.	In 2004: Prod: 49.7 TWh Cons: 49.5 TWh Total imports: 4.1 TWh Total exports: 10.2 TWh Import from Tajikistan 4.1 TWh; imports from Kyrgyzstan 5.8 TWh; exports to Tajikistan 4.7 TWh; export to Afghanistan 0.129 TWh; exports to Kazakhstan 5.3 TWh; exports to Turkmenistan 0.004 TWh. Net importer and expected to increasingly import in future, but could become electricity transit country for Tajik exports. Uzbekistan does not allow transit of Tajik energy to Kazakhstan. It consumes Tajik energy and thereby is able to export its own energy to Kazakhstan at higher prices. In August of 2002 Uzbekistan resumed its supply arrangement to a small area north of Mazar-i-Sharif supplementing a small local gas plant.

Sources: World Bank (2004); "The World Fact Book" (http://www.cia.gov/cia/publications/factbook/geos/af.html); Afghanistan Fact Sheet (http://www.eia.doe.gov/emeu/cabs/afghan.html); "2004 Annual Report" by "ODC Energiya" (Joint Dispatcher Center). CIS Statistics: www.cisstat.com/base/ extrdpred04/21-8.doc; British Petroleum Energy Statistics 2005; Da Afghanistan Breshna Moassessa (DABM, Afghanistan's power utility).

Table A.2. Electricity Trade among Countries in the Wider Central Asia Region and Selected Other Countries (TWhs/year)

Countries (Exporters)	Total Exports	Azer-baijan	Armenia	Belarus	Georgia	Kazakh-stan	Kyrgyz Rep	Moldova	Russia	Tajiki-stan	Turk-meni-stan	Uzbeki-stan	Ukraine	Afghani-stan	Iran
Azerbaijan	238	-	-	-	-	-	-	-	238	-	-	-	-		
Armenia	484	...	-	-	389	-	-	-	-	-	-	-	-		
Belarus	0.4	-	-	-	-	-	-	-	-	-	-	-	0.4		
Georgia	-	-	-	-	-	-	-	-	-	-	-	-	-		
Kazakhstan	7403	-	-	-	-	-	-	-	7403	-	-	-	-		
Kyrgyz Rep	3381	-	-	-	-	1258	-	-	1800	323	-	0.1	-		
Moldova	0.1	-	-	-	-	-	-	-	-	-	-	-	0.1		
Russia	6683	1129	-	1511	798	2272	-	918	-	-	-	-	54		
Tajikistan	4423	-	-	-	-	-	54	-	-	-	-	4369	-		
Turkmenistan	...	...	...	...	...	...	...	...	...	...	-	...	...		
Uzbekistan	...	...	...	...	...	...	...	...	...	...	...	-	...		
Ukraine	852	-	-	0.5	-	-	-	852	-	-	-	-	-		
Afghanistan															
Iran															

Source: CIS Statistics; Afghanistan figures are estimates from DABM for 2003/04.

Given the damaged state of transmission and distribution networks, transmission and distribution (T&D) losses were estimated at 25 percent in 2002. In addition, non-technical losses in the distribution system were estimated at 20 percent. Thus 45 percent of the electricity generated is lost and does not get billed. Only about 54 percent of the value of electricity bills issued is actually collected.

There is no national electricity grid, and the system is made up of four isolated systems centered around the cities of Kabul, Herat, Kandahar, and Mazar-e-Sharif. The largest system is in Kabul, with installed capacity of 245 MW. However, the hydroelectric units have a firm power output of only 65 MW, making electricity shortages more acute in winter. The Afghan power system is connected to those of Tajikistan, Turkmenistan, and Uzbekistan, as shown in Figure A.1, and there are also connections with Iran.

Specifics on some of the more substantial electricity trading connections to Afghanistan (actual or potential) are provided in Table A.3. It is apparent that the cost of imported power for Afghanistan is reasonable and very competitive with short-term or even medium-term generation opportunities in the country. However, the amounts involved are very small, and none of the trade is covered by power purchase agreements (PPAs) or other longer-term contracts. The spatial pattern of existing cross-border electricity interconnections is shown in Figure A.1.

Figure A.1. Afghanistan's Existing Cross-Border Electricity Interconnections

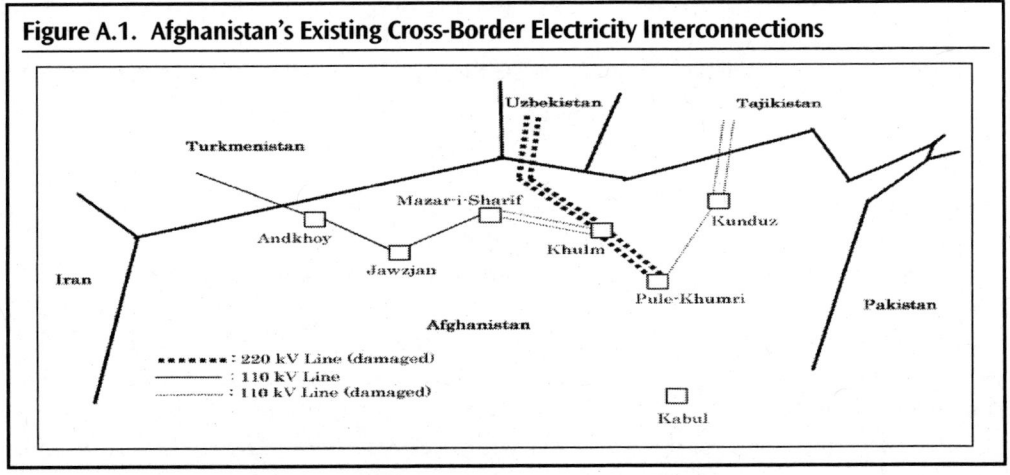

Source: Asian Development Bank, *Study for Power Interconnection for Regional Trade,* March, 2003.

Recent Developments

Existing and planned electricity connections and trade between Afghanistan and its neighbors are outlined below:

- ■ Zabol (Iran)–Zaranj Line: A relatively small link (20 kV single current, between Zabol in Iran and Zaranj in southwest Afghanistan) was opened in March 2004.
- ■ Torbat-e Jam (Iran)–Herat Line: A 132 kV double circuit line from Tobat-e-Jam in Iran to Herat (a 150 km distance) was inaugurated in January 2005.
- ■ Termez (Uzbekistan)–Pul-e-Khumri–Kabul Line: A 220 kV transmission line from Termez via Pul-i-Khumri to Kabul is of crucial importance. Funding for this line

Table A.3. Current Arrangements for Electricity Imports by Afghanistan

	Iran	Tajikistan	Turkmenistan	Uzbekistan
Duration of Contract (years)	4	1	10	1
Maximum Capacity (MW)	2 MW (Nimroz); 2 MW (Herat)	Winter: 5 MW; Summer: Unlimited	2 MW (Herat); 6 MW (Andkhoy)	150
Maximum Energy (million kWh)	NA	NA	15 million kWh	NA
Price (US cents/kWh)	2.25	2	2	2.3

Source: "Central Asia: Regional Electricity Export Potential Study," World Bank, 2004.

has been identified (ADB/India/IDA) and it is envisaged to be completed by March 2007 (Termez–Pul-e-Khumri segment) and October 2008 (Pul-i-Khumri–Kabul).

■ Tajikistan–Pul-e-Khumri Line: 188 km, 2×220 kV also is a promising option. This line is included in an ADB feasibility study and is proposed to be financed in a planned 2007 ADB-financed project that could be completed in late 2008.

■ Sheberghan–Mazar-e-Sharif: 142 km, 220 kV line is being assessed as part of an ADB feasibility study and is proposed for funding in the same planned ADB-financed project.

■ Afghanistan–Pakistan lines: Although there are no existing connections, according to news reports Afghanistan has requested connections and imports of electricity into the border provinces of Khost, Paktia, and Paktika.

It should also be noted that ongoing and planned investments in electricity transmission lines are being financed by several donors using different implementing agencies, carrying a risk of uneven progress of implementation and possible confusion. Figure A.2 shows the pattern of financing and planned completion dates for priority transmission lines to and in northern Afghanistan and extending down to Kabul. Clearly there is an urgent need to accelerate and coordinate these projects and to move quickly to secure funding for those that are yet unfunded.

Overall, these initiatives for short-run imports of electricity into Afghanistan are promising and in some cases have already yielded beneficial results for parts of Afghanistan. However, progress has been slow on some of the more substantial efforts, reflecting infrastructure constraints, slow project implementation (due to, among other constraints, security issues in Afghanistan), and inability to formalize agreements on power supply in some cases.

Way Forward

In order to expand and accelerate progress in importing electricity from neighboring countries into Afghanistan, specific action programs are needed along the following lines involving Afghanistan, its neighbors, and external partners providing financing:

■ *Formalize power purchase agreements as needed.* In particular, concluding a long-term power purchase agreement (PPA) between Uzbekistan and Afghanistan is a

Figure A.2. Priority Transmission Lines

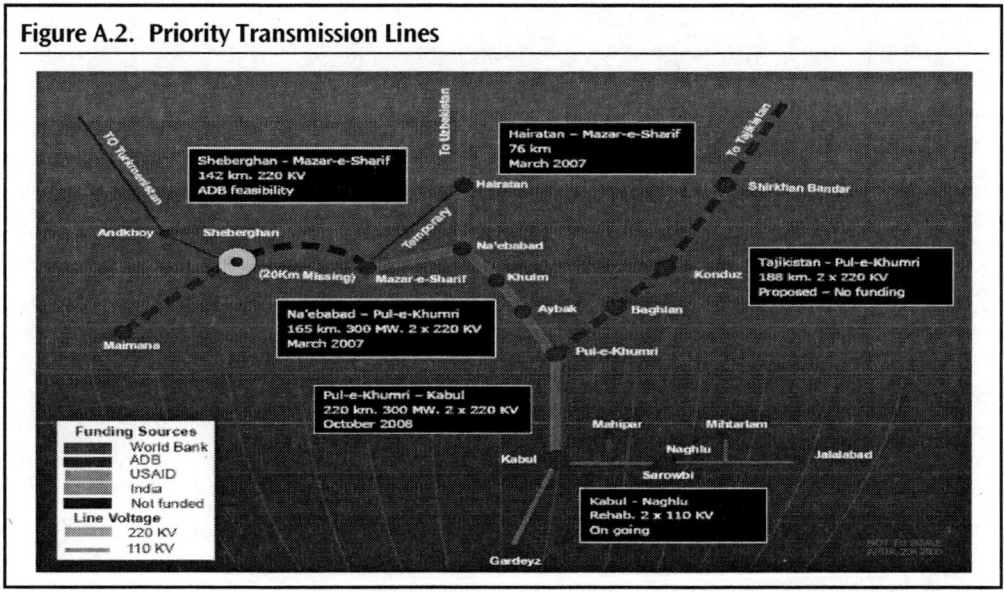

priority in the near future. In other cases, PPAs may be useful to regularize existing power trading arrangements and provide stability for both the demand and the supply side.

▪ *Ensure that payments do not become a bottleneck.* This will require improved utility finances and management in Afghanistan, including cost recovery where it is currently inadequate, notably in Kabul. Suitable payment guarantee mechanisms may also be worth considering.

▪ *Accelerated construction of transmission infrastructure.* Additional measures need to be taken to ensure that construction of transmission lines occurs in a timely manner and meets deadlines. Stronger management and coordination by the Afghan Government's Ministry of Energy and Water (MoEW)—which could be based on a technically qualified, strongly supported focal point—is required to ensure that administrative bottlenecks are quickly resolved, gaps filled, and on-the-ground obstacles overcome. Donors should pro-actively support Government leadership in this regard, including by ensuring that financing gaps for critical transmission projects are filled.

Options for Pursuing More Substantial "Breakthrough" Projects

There are sites in the mountainous parts of the wider Central Asia region with large hydroelectric potential, ranging up to 4,000 MW capacity. There is, as will be explored in more detail in the next section, high demand for power to the south, north, and west of the region as well as within it. Thus there are clear opportunities for large-scale production and trade in electricity across substantial distances in and around the region. The medium-term prospects are therefore very promising, and for the same reasons there are also investment opportunities for specific "breakthrough" projects that could tap a discrete chunk of the potential on an accelerated basis. In addition to their substantial financial and economic returns, such projects would have a powerful demonstration effect and would build a solid track record and strong momentum for further progress. Thus although they would require considerably more time and resources—financial, technical, administrative, and political—and moreover carry significant risks, such opportunities appear to be very much worth pursuing.

A notable example, which has already received considerable attention, is the Sangtuda I hydropower project, a partially constructed run-of-the-river facility on the Vakhsh River (an Amu Darya tributary) in Tajikistan. This project would have a capacity of 670 MW, and its output could be supplied to Pakistan via Afghanistan. There is strong private sector interest in this project, along with interest on the part of the governments of the three concerned countries. The key challenge—technically, financially, implementation-wise, and in terms of contracting, organization, and regulation—would be the transmission lines, including the challenge of security in some of the areas they would pass through. Determining the level and seasonal pattern of export potential also would be very important.

Medium-Term Prospects for Electricity Trade

Supply Options

Focusing on electricity, which in its primary form consists of hydropower and in secondary form thermal generation, supply options to meet existing and future demand include the following: (i) projects for rehabilitation of the transmission and distribution system to reduce the high level of Transmission and Distribution (T&D) losses; (ii) projects for rehabilitating existing generating units; and (iii) construction of new generating plants.

All of the countries in the region, as well as surrounding countries with large potential demand for power, suffer from substantial T&D losses, whose reduction would augment effective power supply (see Table A.4). This will require investments in distribution rehabilitation, reinforcements, and expansion. Taking the four countries in former-Soviet Central Asia (excluding Turkmenistan) as an example, loss reduction projects during 2005–2010

Table A.4. Current and Targeted Electricity Loss Levels in Selected Countries

Country	Current Losses* (%) (2004)	Target Loss Levels (%)	Time Period of the Projects	Additional Annual Electricity (GWh) in 2010
Kazakhstan	24	15	2004–2010	5,843
Kyrgyz Republic	34	13	2004–2010	1,392[15]
Tajikistan	28	13	2004–2010	1,988
Uzbekistan	25	15	2004–2010	4,064
Turkmenistan				
Afghanistan	45**	n/a		

*Includes technical losses mainly, but also some commercial (unbilled consumption) losses.
**Very rough estimate.
Source: World Bank (2004).

---

15. An additional 220 GWh would be realized in 2011.

would make available additional supply of more than 13 TWh of electricity on an annual basis. This compares with total supply by these countries of about 146 TWh in 2004.

There are also some options to augment electricity supply through rehabilitation of generation facilities, mainly thermal plants in Uzbekistan and Kazakhstan. In Uzbekistan there are several short-run rehabilitation investments underway. It is roughly estimated that rehabilitation of power plants over the next two decades, costing US$1.15 billion, would extend the life of power plants and avoid the loss of around 32,000 GWh of total generation (during 2005–2025) due to retirements of capacity that would otherwise occur. In the case of Kazakhstan, some major coal-fired power generation facilities are operating at low plant utilization factors, and it has been estimated that a total investment of roughly $1.07 billion would extend the operational lives of units and improve their plant load factor, resulting in incremental generation of 17,000 GWh.

Major new power generation projects comprise a more substantial, costly option for increasing electricity supplies, requiring sizable investments and time to reap returns. Again taking the four countries in former Soviet Central Asia as an example, Table A.5 shows estimated power supply costs from new power generation options, including both thermal and hydel projects. The economic and financial costs of supply for most of these projects compare favorably with marginal generation costs in target export markets, which are estimated at 3.0 cents/kwh in Russia, 3.6 cents/kwh in Iran, 3.7 cents/kwh in Afghanistan, 3.6–4.0 cents/kwh in China, and as high as 5.6 cents/kwh in Pakistan.

If all of the rehabilitation and new generation projects discussed above are implemented, the overall gross power supply in all four countries would rise from 139 TWh in 2003 to 228 TWh in 2025. About 54 percent of this incremental supply would come from new generating units, about 16 percent from loss reduction programs, and the remaining 30 percent from rehabilitation of old generating units. Kazakhstan would contribute 45 percent of the incremental supply, followed by Uzbekistan and Tajikistan (22 percent each) and the Kyrgyz Republic (9 percent). The Kyrgyz Republic and Tajikistan also have some additional options to increase the availability of electricity in winter from existing sources: (i) in the Kyrgyz Republic, it is now possible to operate Toktogul cascade in a modified irrigation mode which will enable the release of an additional 1.5 BCM of water and thus generate an additional 1.5 billion kWh in the winter; and (ii) in Tajikistan it is possible to shift heating demand away from electricity to other resources (coal, gas, biomass), which is expected to make available roughly 860 GWh to meet electricity demand.

Rough forecasts of available electricity surpluses for the four countries indicate that if the investments discussed go ahead, there will be large surpluses available for export, albeit with Kazakhstan projected to go into deficit after 2020 (see Table A.6). The table also highlights that there will be tremendous seasonal variation, with large surpluses available in the summer immediately and further growing over the next decade.

Sources of Demand

In addition to Afghanistan's requirements in the short run (described earlier), there is expected to be large demand for surplus power generated in Central Asia in coming years—from South Asia (Pakistan and India), Russia, and Iran. Moreover, Kazakhstan itself is expected to turn into a net importer of electricity by the year 2020. Gaps can be predicted only roughly, but they would appear to be large enough to absorb prospective surplus power

Table A.5. Supply Costs from Generation Options

No.	Country	Supply Option	Capacity in MW	Economic Cost/kWh in Cents	Financial Cost/kWh in Cents	National System Marginal Supply Cost/kwh in Cents
1	Uzbekistan	Talimardjan Thermal Power Project I	800	1.68	1.75	3.5
2		Talimardjan Thermal Power Project II	2,400	2.76	2.92	3.5
3	Kyrgyz Republic	Bishkek II Thermal Power Project	400	2.55	2.67	2.3
4		Kambarata Hydropower Project I	1,900	7.17	8.54	2.3
5		Kambarata Hydropower Project II	360	3.72	3.95	2.3
6	Tajikistan	Sangtuda I Hydropower Project	670	1.97	2.44	2.1
7		Rogun Hydropower Project Phase I	1,200	2.46	2.91	2.1
8		Rogun Hydropower Project Phases I and II	3,600	2.83	3.24	2.1
9	Kazakhstan	New Ekibastuz Thermal Power Project	1,000	4.54	5.05	2.8
	Turkmenistan					
	Afghanistan*	Sheberghan Gas Power Project	100	n/a	n/a	n/a
		Baghdara Hydropower Project	280	n/a	n/a	n/a

*Feasibility studies just getting underway.
Source: World Bank (2004).

Table A.6. Surplus Electricity Available for Trade (GWh), Annual and Seasonal

Country	Season	2005	2010	2015	2020	2025
Kazakhstan	Summer	3198	3623	6876	3745	−234
	Winter	−2504	−2969	−130	−5563	−12318
	Annual	694	654	6746	−1818	−12552
Kyrgyz Republic	Summer	4737	6283	6863	6406	5991
	Winter	−2092	1584	1517	5761	4753
	Annual	2645	7866	8381	12167	10744
Tajikistan	Summer	1511	4587	6767	12579	11697
	Winter	96	2841	4287	8308	7431
	Annual	1607	7429	11055	20887	19128
Uzbekistan	Summer	1620	3904	7635	5088	2091
	Winter	2862	5485	9846	7058	3767
	Annual	4482	9389	17481	12147	5858
All 4 CA Countries	Summer	11066	18396	28142	27819	19545
	Winter	−1637	6942	15521	15564	3633
	Annual	9429	25338	43663	43383	23178
	Winter					
	Annual					

Source: World Bank (2004).

from Central Asia. Available information, summarized in Table A.5 and for selected options in Table A.7, suggests that meeting such gaps through electricity imports would be cost-effective as a medium-term option.

Constraints and Risks

As indicated in Chapter 2 of this paper, energy development and trade are subject to serious constraints. For electricity trade, short-run obstacles include most notably lack of transmission connections as well as, in the case of Afghanistan, extremely limited distribution infrastructure which severely limits grid demand. While some short connections have already been made and more are possible, there are serious bottlenecks in terms of power transmission to and within Afghanistan. For example, the major transmission line from the northern border with Uzbekistan south to Kabul has taken much longer than originally expected to complete, mainly due to delays in finalizing financing arrangements. Over the medium term, sizable transmission investments would be required to enable large-scale regularized electricity trade. In addition, longer-term power purchase agreements (PPAs) would be required, and an effective regulatory framework would need to be functioning, requiring institutional development and capacity building in the countries concerned as well as multilateral agreements (since large-scale trade would almost invariably involve three or more countries).

The main risks associated with regional electricity trade of a substantial scale, along with possible mitigation measures, are outlined in Table A.8. In addition, security along

Table A.7. Marginal Costs of Generation in Target Markets versus Import Costs (cents/kWh)

Target Market	Marginal Generation Cost in Target Market	Supply Options	Transmission Cost	Total Delivered Cost of Imports
Afghanistan	3.7	Sangtuda I, Rogun I, Talimardjan I and II	0.51	2.26–3.43
Iran	3.6	Sangtuda I, Rogun I, Talimardjan I and II	0.54	2.29–3.46
Pakistan	5.6	Sangtuda I, Rogun Talimardjan I and II, Kambarata II	0.51	2.26–3.75
India		*Some projects from Pakistan and Afghanistan could potentially be economically viable as an export option to India.*		

Source: World Bank (2004); staff estimates.

transmission routes is a risk in the region, particularly those going through Afghanistan. Among the options to mitigate security risks are, at a minimum, ensuring that there is electric power available to communities situated along the routes of the transmission lines, and also local, community, and rural development initiatives in these areas (perhaps including activities that benefit from the availability of power and local resources).

Moving Forward

This paper has argued that there is great potential for regionally-oriented development of the electricity sector in the wider Central Asia region. Although the constraints are very

Table A.8. Risks and Mitigation Measures

Risk	Mitigation
Supply security due to import/ transit dependency	• Diversification of supply and fuel mix • Economic cooperation has a positive feedback on political relationships
Contract enforcement and payment risks	• Need to improve arbitration, regional banking (payment securities)
Pricing policies	• Harmonize regulation, improve subsidization policies
Balance of payment exposure	• Improve regional pricing, risk sharing, develop hedging opportunities and instruments
Infrastructural bottlenecks	• Improve regional planning • Harmonize infrastructure access regulation

Source: Presentation on South Asia Regional Energy Trade: Opportunities and Challenges (World Bank Annual Meetings, October 1, 2004).

real, there are promising opportunities—more than in most other sectors—for progress in the short run, both through modest win-win initiatives for electricity trade (in particular small and medium-scale exports to Afghanistan) that in several cases are already underway, and through more substantial projects on which thinking is already advanced in some cases. Success on both of these fronts would build a track record, momentum, and political buy-in for more ambitious actions over time toward coordinated development of electricity resources and trade.

In fact, strategic thinking and coalescence of views of different countries on the approach to regional electric power development and appropriate sequencing have advanced considerably in the region. Most notably, a major meeting on electricity held by ECO in 2005 agreed on a broad strategy for electricity development in the ECO region and its neighborhood, which incorporates both short-term and medium-term aspects. As summarized in Box A.1, the approach involves: (i) pursuing specific regional projects including both modest electricity exports to Afghanistan and potentially larger "win-win" projects; (ii) undertaking analytical work on the long-term potential for power development in the region; (iii) encouraging the exchange of information; and (iv) creating an institutional and organizational framework for advancing the regional electricity (and broader energy) agenda.

Sustained followup, as well as building and maintaining momentum, will be key to moving forward along the lines of the approach agreed at the ECO meeting. While the opportunities are clear, successfully exploiting them will require political buy-in and active

---

Box A.1. Regional Approach to Electricity Development Agreed by ECO

At an important meeting of ECO in 2005 on electricity, a strategy was agreed which has four main elements, articulated and developed below:

First, *pursue specific regional projects* (bilateral, multilateral, within the region, or between the region and its neighborhood) which can be identified quickly as potentially win-win and economic; one such project potentially is the export of electricity from Tajikistan to Afghanistan and Pakistan, based on existing surpluses and the Sangtuda-I hydropower plant, with options to expand it further, possibly to Sangtuda-II and Rogun, and surpluses from Kyrgyzstan; another is exports from Iran to Pakistan; yet another is from Pakistan to the border regions of Afghanistan; and there may be more such options in and around the region—Iran-Turkmenistan, Iran-Tajikistan, Armenia-Iran, Turkey-Georgia, and so forth.

Second, *undertake analytical work* which would examine longer-term potential, its costs and benefits, opportunities and constraints.

Third, *encourage exchange of information* among the countries concerned, starting by establishing a "data center," initially with the ECO Secretariat.

Fourth, *create an institutional and organizational framework* for advancing regional energy trade. At the organizational level, this could take a form of region-wide permanent working group(s) on energy cooperation. An initial structure could involve a steering group at the political/policy level, plus a technical working group. At the institutional level, the region could start with some sort of Energy Charter (like the European Energy Charter), which is basically a multilateral inter-governmental agreement on facilitating energy transit, trade, cross-border investment, and settlement of disputes; and then transit toward more common-energy-market arrangements, of which, for example, a coordinated regional electricity pool is an ultimate form.

leadership from the countries concerned, administrative support and capacity (if necessary brought in on an extraordinary basis) in the governments of these countries, and technical and financial support as needed from donors. Regional organizations need to take a pro-active role on a sustained basis, including follow-up by ECO after its successful meeting. Creating a lean but effective regional institutional and organizational framework for power development/trade, as agreed at the ECO meeting, will support follow-up and help ensure sustained progress.

Momentum has begun to be built up through intensive discussions and meetings on possible "breakthrough" projects. However, for such initiatives to successfully move forward, putting the required conditions in place needs to be given high priority by the governments of the countries concerned. Construction of transmission lines through Afghanistan will not be easy and will require concerted efforts and high-level attention. Contracting arrangements for large-scale electricity supply and trade will be technically complex, with multiple countries and the private sector involved.

In the case of smaller-scale electricity imports into Afghanistan, a track record and momentum are emerging. As discussed earlier, key priorities include: (i) formalizing power purchase agreements as needed; (ii) ensuring that payments do not become a bottleneck; and (iii) accelerating construction of necessary transmission infrastructure. Such arrangements can provide a foundation for deeper and larger-scale cooperation over time.

Finally, as indicated in Box A.1, further analytical work—explicitly taking a fully regional perspective—is a high priority, to:

- Examine and quantify the economic potential for increasing cross-border electricity trade and investment, and assess the associated costs and benefits.
- Identify barriers to regional energy cooperation and make recommendations to reduce or remove them.
- Identify and prioritize electricity investment projects of regional significance.
- Describe options for financing and implementing regional electricity projects and the role which various stakeholders could play (public and private sectors, international financial institutions, etc.).
- Develop recommendations for the policy makers on how to create a conducive environment for increased intra- and inter-regional electricity trade and investment.
- Propose a roadmap for dealing with policy, institutional, regulatory, commercial, technical, environmental, and social issues in pursuing regional energy cooperation.

Bringing the Region Closer Together Through Transport Connections

Central Asia's potential as a land bridge between East and West was most developed during the 3rd to 16th centuries—the heyday of the famous Silk Road (albeit with significant interruptions during this period, due to conflicts and periods of economic isolation of different civilizations and empires). However, with the decline of the caravan trade and the growing importance of maritime transportation, the Silk Road languished. Today, Central Asia's strategic location at the crossroads of major overland trading routes does not translate into major economic benefits, and its long distance from the sea is a major disadvantage. Afghanistan was especially isolated as a landlocked country during the more than two decades of conflict and resulting destruction of infrastructure and associated security concerns. Uzbekistan is one of only two doubly landlocked countries in the world (doubly because all of its neighbors also are landlocked). Kazakhstan has the longest distance from the sea in the world (3,750 km; Ojala 2004). As long as transport routes through Afghanistan are not developed, Tajikistan, itself a doubly landlocked country, is in the unenviable position of having to communicate with the rest of the world via another doubly landlocked country, namely Uzbekistan. In addition, it is internally divided by mountain ranges, and the main North-South roads are closed for five months of the year. Kyrgyzstan is similarly cut in half, and dependent for access to world markets on available routes via Kazakhstan.

This Appendix discusses key issues and options for improving transport connections within and through the Wider Central Asia region. The first section summarizes research findings on the costs of being landlocked, a situation faced by a number of regional countries and large parts of the territory of the region. The second section reviews existing data and analysis on transport costs along existing routes to Europe from post-Soviet Central Asia. The costs of proposed new routes through Afghanistan are discussed in the subsequent section. Issues related to transport costs between Afghanistan, Iran and Pakistan also are discussed in this context. The fourth section points out assumptions made and knowledge gaps which need to be addressed, and the fifth section puts forward some recommendations for short-term action.

The Costs of Being Landlocked

The negative effects of a country being landlocked include increased prices for essential imports and reduced export revenues due to disproportionately high transportation costs. Neighboring countries attempt to collect transit rents, and if trade and transit policies remain uncoordinated, transportation costs increase by disproportionately more than the distance to target markets. Existing studies demonstrate that freight costs of landlocked countries account for about 15 percent of the value of imports (c.i.f.) compared to about 7 percent and 4 percent for other developing and developed countries respectively. Similarly, landlocked countries tend to spend about 18 percent of their export revenues on freight and insurance, in comparison to 9 percent in other developing countries (U.N. 2001). For the countries of Central Asia, these estimates would imply freight costs in the range of 14 percent of GDP (Table B.1).

Table B.1. Estimated Freight Costs for the Countries of Central Asia

Country	GDP (US$ billion)	Exports (US$ billion)	X as % of GDP %	Imports (US$ billion)	M as % of GDP %	Freight Costs (US$ billion)	Freight Costs % of GDP
Kazakhstan	41	18	45%	16	40%	5.7	14%
Uzbekistan	12	5	39%	4	31%	1.4	12%
Turkmenistan	6	4	62%	3	54%	1.2	19%
Afghanistan	5	0.6	12%	3	69%	0.6	13%
Kyrgyz Rep	2	1	42%	1	51%	0.3	15%
Tajikistan	2	1	55%	1	65%	0.4	20%
Total:	68	29	44%	29	42%	9.6	14%

Source: World Bank staff calculations.

Recent studies furthermore suggest that over the period 1960–92, landlocked developing countries on average grew at rates 1.5 percent per year slower than countries that were not landlocked (McKellar, Worgotter, and Worz 2000). In a similar vein, research by the United Nations indicates that landlocked countries tend to have lower levels of human development, higher rates of labor migration, and associated losses due to brain drain (although this can be offset by gains due to remittances and return migration).[16] In Cen-

---

16. For a detailed discussion of migration issues in Europe and Central Asia, see the flagship study on migration prepared by the World Bank (2005d).

tral Asia, being landlocked is estimated to reduce trade by more then 80 percent, primarily because of the costs of crossing borders and land-transit through neighboring countries rather than due to geographical distance to destination markets *per se* (Raballand 2003). Concretely, Tajikistan is presently cut off from major road transit routes due to the prohibitive costs of road transit through Uzbekistan. Afghanistan faces restrictions (although recently reduced to a small list) on the kinds of goods allowed to transit through Pakistan, while the transit for instance of Indian exports to Afghanistan and Central Asia through Pakistan is virtually blocked.[17] Kyrgyz and Uzbek trucks pay US$1,500–2,000 in transit through Kazakhstan to Russia, most of this as informal payments to the road police. Finally, Limão and Venables (1999) estimate that halving transport costs of a landlocked country increases the volume of trade by a factor of five. Therefore, there are significant potential gains from reducing the cost of trade and transit, including by creating alternative transport corridors to compete with the existing ones.

The policy-induced costs of transportation are further discussed in Appendix C. However, physical obstacles related to the nature of the terrain and the quality of infrastructure clearly are important as well. Nevertheless, as discussed below, the much shorter distance of trading routes from Central Asia to Iran and Pakistan through Afghanistan should make these routes attractive. At present they are not, largely because of security concerns, high costs, and long delays. There are thus large potential gains from reducing the costs of trade and transit to, from, and through the region.

Existing Transport Corridors

While culturally and historically, wider Central Asia may be regarded as a closely connected region, the existing transport infrastructure strongly reflects the historical legacies of British–Russian confrontation and the subsequent Cold War divisions on the Eurasian continent. The Soviet road and railway infrastructure was oriented toward Russia. For the post-Soviet Republics of Central Asia this northern route still dominates. However, new routes through Iran and Turkey (west) and to China (east) are being developed, driven by growing trade relations with these countries.

The southern route through Afghanistan remains underdeveloped., There are no rail links from the south and east into Afghanistan and no transit connection from post-Soviet Central Asia to Pakistan and India through Afghanistan, although a railway link through Turkmenistan to Iran and the port at Bandar Abbas was opened in 1997. The reconstruction of road links through Afghanistan has made considerable progress but has been impeded by security concerns, which continue to slow down civil works. Ojala (2005) indicates that the value of total exports shipped from post-Soviet Central Asia via Afghanistan may not have exceeded US$170 million, including transit to Pakistan and India. This compares to US$480 million through Iran by road (and another US$630 million by rail) and US$800 million to China by road (US$ 1 billion by rail). For the northern and western routes, the figures are considerably higher.

---

17. India's growing trade with Central Asia presently goes almost entirely through Iran's Bandar-Abbas port or by air freight through Dubai. See Ojala (2005).

Equally important, Central Asia's major neighbors—China, India, Iran, and Russia—have direct links with each other, bypassing the region. Russia trades with Iran and the Gulf directly through the Caspian Sea or through Azerbaijan. China can trade with Pakistan and the Indian Ocean through the Karakorum Highway by land, and also directly by the shipping route through the Malaysian straits.

Existing studies of the costs of different transportation corridors are largely based on surveys of freight forwarders. For routes that are in regular use, these provide reasonably robust estimates and show some interesting changes over time. However, for the North-South routes through Afghanistan reliable estimates are rare. Hence comparison of transport and transit costs along different routes is beset with difficulties, and additional analytical work will be required to obtain more robust estimates.

Ojala (2005) provides a comparison of transport costs (both in US$ and also in transit time) by road, rail, and air from different locations in post-Soviet Central Asia (Table B.2). As is evident, rail transportation is considerably cheaper than road but takes considerably longer. Air freight is obviously fastest but at costs between US$1800–2100 per ton is clearly

Table B.2. Estimated Transport Costs from Europe to Central Asia and other CIS Capitals

	Dushanbe (TAJ)	Khujan (TAJ)	Tashkent (UZB)	Almaty (KAZ)	Bishkek (KGZ)	Ashgabat (TKM)	Baku (AZE)	Tbilisi (GEO)	Yerevan (ARM)
40' Container by Road Transport									
Typical Transit Time	15	14	12	13	14	14	13	12	14
Ojala Spring 2004	9200	9000	7000	8000		8000	7000	6000	7000
Raballand 2004*			4000						
Ojala Spring 2005	7500	7000	5500	5500	6500	n.a.	6000	5000	6500
40' Container by Rail									
Typical Transit Time	28	26	23	21	24	28	24	24	30
Ojala Spring 2004	3400	3000	2800	3000		3300	2700	2500	2800
Raballand 2004*			4000						
Ojala Spring 2005	3400	3200	3000	3000	3100	2900	3000	3000	3300
A Small Shipper Exporting 1 ton by Road Freight									
Typical Transit Time	19	19	14	14	16	17	15	14	18
Ojala Spring 2004	500	480	300	300		400	280	300	420
Ojala Spring 2005	430	400	320	300	350	n.a.	300	300	360
1 ton by Air Freight									
Typical Transit Time	6	6	4	4	5	6	5	5	6
Ojala Spring 2004	2400	2200	2000	2100		2300	2100	2000	2300
Ojala Spring 2005	2100	2000	1800	1800	2000	2300	2000	2000	2300

Source: Ojala (2005), p. 27; Ojala's data are from Belgium/Netherlands and include unofficial payments. Raballand's data are to Paris. Both sources are based on surveys of freight forwarders.

attractive only for the highest-value goods.[18] Costs of road and air transportation seem to have fallen since 2004 by around 15 percent on average, whereas rail transport costs have remained roughly the same. Because tonnage shipped by road and air on the route to Europe has been increasing in recent years, this could be indicative of growing competition. In the absence of concrete data on market structure, however, this is largely speculative. Table B.2 also reveals the considerable cost added by border crossings; for example, costs from Khujand (a mere 250 km from Tashkent) are US$1,500–2,000 above costs from Tashkent. Similarly, road costs from Bishkek are around US$1,000 above costs from Almaty. Interestingly, similar rents do not seem to be collected on rail routes, although crossing an additional border in Central Asia adds on average a full three days to the length of a rail journey.

Table B.2 also records transit costs and times to Europe via Russia. This is not the shortest but still the most frequently used route. The alternative routes to Europe by road (including routes through Russia) are:

- Northern Route (via Russia, Belarus, and Poland): 5790 km
- Southern Route (via Iran and Turkey): 7000 km
- TRACECA via the Caspian and Black Sea: 6000–6250 km
- Pan European Corridor (via Russia, Ukraine, and Poland): 4600 km

Kazakhstan predominantly uses the Northern Route, whereas Uzbekistan increasingly uses the Southern Route. Compared to these European routes, Southern routes to the Persian Gulf or the Indian Ocean are clearly much shorter, and potentially highly competitive. Add to this the present imbalance in most shipments by road, whereby trucks enter Central Asia well loaded but leave virtually empty, and truckers from Iran and Turkey potentially could offer very competitive rates. In an ideal world, a typical 40 ton truckload could reach Teheran for US$3,000 round trip and Bandar-Abbas for perhaps US$4,000. In practice, the round trip to Teheran costs US$5,000 and to Bandar-Abbas around US$6,000, with most of the extra cost attributable to informal payments. Based on current freight loads in Pakistan and if these were recognized by the Central Asian countries, the land route to Karachi would be even more competitive, but transit cargo takes on average around two weeks from Karachi to Tashkent, compared to 7–9 days from Bandar-Abbas and around 15 days from Europe. So far, therefore, neither of the two Southern routes is much in use.

The picture is similar for transportation by rail, as Table B.3 reveals. In principle, the southern railway link to Bandar-Abbas is considerably shorter than any of the Western or Northern routes. Because of long delays at the Turkmenistan border and further delays during transhipment at the Iranian border due to a change in gauges, this route remains under-utilized, although its use has been increasing recently.[19] The construction of the Bafq-Mashhad rail link will further reduce the distance on this route and may make it com-

---

18. At present this would include primarily imports of perishable consumer goods for which value/weight ratios are high and transport time is critical. On the export side, air freight could be attractive for cut flowers, highly seasonal fruit and vegetables (e.g. for the winter markets in Moscow), and shipments of gold. There is significant potential to develop such exports since at present most planes bringing freight into Central Asia leave empty, although this would require the development of a more market-oriented and competitive freight forwarding industry.

19. More than half of Uzbekistan's cotton exports are now estimated to be shipped by rail through Bandar-Abbas.

Table B.3. Existing Railway Links Between Central Asia and Major Ports

Origin	Destination Seaport	Distance
Almaty	Aktau-Baku-Poti (Black Sea)	4600
	Novorossiysk (Black Sea)	4630
	Bandar Abbas (Persian Gulf)	4800 (3770*)
	Riga (Baltic Sea)	5350
	Druzhba-Shanghai (Pacific)	5370
	Mersin (Mediterranean Sea)	5421
	Vladivastok (Pacific)	7850
Tashkent	Bandar Abbas (Persian Gulf)	3800 (2770*)
	Aktau-Baku-Poti (Black Sea)	3900
	Novorossiysk (Black Sea)	3950
	Mersin (Mediterranean Sea)	4421
	Riga (Baltic Sea)	5500
	Druzhba-Shanghai (Pacific)	6320
	Vladivastok (Pacific)	8800

*After the completion of Mashad-Bafq railway section in Iran.
Source: "Transit Transport Issues in Landlocked and Transit Developing Countries," United Nations, 2003.

petitive with European routes in the future. But the key constraint appears to be the time required to cross borders.

Evidence on the costs of official and unofficial barriers to trade and transit from Afghanistan through Iran and Pakistan is scantier than for post-Soviet Central Asia. For a 40-foot container from Karachi, quoted costs to Kabul or Kandahar are around US$3,000. This is comprised of around two-thirds pure transport costs and the remainder of expenditures on port charges, customs, unloading and reloading charges, and road tolls. To this, informal payments to customs and for road security need to be added, for which no precise estimates are available from existing sources. Yet, the most important costs incurred are due to time delays, with transit through Pakistan to Kabul taking around 20 days by road and rail, or 14 days by road alone, of which four days is in Afghanistan. Transit by road from Iran is more expensive but saves around eight days on the journey. Increasing the speed of transit through Afghanistan is therefore key to developing trade and transit on the North-South corridors.

The geographical orientation of trade from the region reflects the North-South bifurcation of transport systems (Table B.4 and Table B.5). While trade from post-Soviet Central Asia with Iran and China has been picking up in recent years, trade with Afghanistan and Pakistan is still minimal. Even India represents barely 1 percent of the total trade of the region. By contrast, trade relations between Afghanistan and Pakistan have traditionally been vibrant, as have been Afghanistan's trade relations with Iran. A particularly interesting aspect of trade within the wider Central Asia region is the fact that while among the Central Asian republics intra-regional trade is quite small, once the major regional neighbors such as China, Iran, Pakistan, and Russia are added, the share of intra-regional trade in total trade with wider Central Asia reaches more than half in many cases. This is quite unlike many developing countries and also unlike other transition economies in eastern Europe, whose main trading partners are OECD countries. This demonstrates that Central Asia truly lies at the crossroads of the spheres of influence of several regional powers. The promise of greater cooperation in

Table B.4. Imports (CIF, $US millions) within Wider Central Asia as a Share of Total Regional Imports (2004)

Imports from:	Imports (as reported by importers) by: ($US millions)															Total All	X*
	AFG	KAZ	KGZ	TJK	TKM	UZB	CA	IRN	PAK	RUS	WCA	CHN	IND	TUR	UAE		
Afghanistan	0	0	0	4	0	0	4	0	49	4	58	1	43	7	4	113	103
Kazakhstan	71	0	230	153	101	199	754	588	1	3,457	4,800	2,286	14	441	8	7,550	7,061
Kyrgyz Republic	8	73	0	18	8	24	129	3	0	150	282	110	1	13	26	431	559
Tajikistan	8	4	4	0	8	73	97	33	8	76	213	15	4	63	0	296	320
Turkmenistan	107	64	1	34	0	16	221	727	9	43	1,000	14	10	176	136	1,336	1,161
Uzbekistan	0	118	51	169	60	0	398	83	6	612	1,099	403	29	179	0	1,709	1,559
Total Imports from CA	194	259	286	377	177	311	1,604	1,433	73	4,342	7,452	2,829	101	878	175	11,435	10,763
Imports from CA as % of the total imports	10%	2%	21%	32%	6%	10%	6%	4%	0%	6%	5%	1%	0%	1%	0%	1%	1%
Iran	0	17	9	26	123	0	175	0	272	111	559	4,492	366	1,961	438	7,815	6,982
Pakistan	511	10	6	0	1	3	531	113	0	25	669	595	86	240	1,080	2,670	2,275
Russia	84	5,113	300	241	267	844	6,847	2,081	222	0	9,150	12,129	1,189	9,027	530	32,025	28,462
Total imports from WCA	789	5,398	600	644	568	1,158	9,157	3,627	567	4,478	17,829	20,045	1,742	12,107	2,224	53,946	48,482
as % of the total imports	39%	37%	45%	54%	21%	37%	36%	9%	3%	6%	12%	4%	2%	12%	3%	5%	5%
China	64	2,269	352	57	94	183	3,019	2,762	1,499	4,733	12,014	0	6,073	4,464	7,396	29,947	32,787
India	170	86	39	3	17	20	336	1,253	455	643	2,686	7,677	0	1,046	7,265	18,675	13,976
Turkey	78	391	72	38	236	160	975	891	90	1,225	3,181	591	115	0	1,253	5,141	5,325

(continued)

Table B.4. Imports (CIF, $US millions) within Wider Central Asia as a Share of Total Regional Imports (2004) (Continued)

Imports from:	Imports (as reported by importers) by: ($US millions)															Total All	X*
	AFG	KAZ	KGZ	TJK	TKM	UZB	CA	IRN	PAK	RUS	WCA	CHN	IND	TUR	UAE		
United Arab Emirates	5	33	9	16	252	0	317	2,757	1,773	14	4,860	1,304	3,951	182	0	10,298	9,351
Total imports from WCA plus neighbors	1,106	8,178	1,072	759	1,168	1,521	13,803	11,290	4,383	11,093	40,570	29,618	11,881	17,799	18,138	118,007	109,921
as % of the total imports	55%	55%	80%	64%	43%	48%	55%	30%	25%	16%	27%	5%	12%	18%	24%	12%	10%
Total Imports (World)	2,002	14,776	1,341	1,191	2,737	3,144	25,190	38,257	17,756	69,055	150,258	561,422	99,833	97,337	74,268	983,119	1,048,152

*Exports. The exports for Wider CA are as reported by exporters (see table B5). Consequently discrepancies may be due to under-reporting of exports as well as to transport costs accounting for differences between fob export and cif import values.

Source: IMF Directions of Trade Statistics.

Table B.5.   Exports (FOB, $US millions) within Wider Central Asia as a Share of Total Regional Exports (2004)

Exports to:	Exports (as reported by exporters) by:															Wider CA & neighbors
	AFG	KAZ	KGZ	TJK	TKM	UZB	CA	IRN	PAK	RUS	WCA	CHN	IND	TUR	UAE	
Afghanistan		65	7	8	97	0	176	0	465	76	717	57	154	71	4	1003
Kazakhstan	0		78	4	4	107	193	15	9	4648	4865	2212	78	356	30	7541
Kyrgyz Republic	0	191		4	1	46	242	8	5	265	521	493	46	75	9	1143
Tajikistan	4	139	17		31	153	343	24	0	183	551	54	6	42	15	666
Turkmenistan	0	49	3	8		55	115	112	1	242	470	85	16	215	229	1015
Uzbekistan	0	181	22	66	14		283	0	3	767	1053	172	19	145	0	1389
Total exports to CA	4	624	127	89	147	362	1353	159	483	6181	8177	3073	319	903	287	12758
as % of the total exports	2%	3%	18%	10%	4%	14%	5%	0%	4%	4%	3%	1%	0%	1%	0%	1%
Iran	0	535	3	30	661	75	1303		103	1892	3298	2555	1139	810	2506	10308
Pakistan	45	1	0	0	8	6	60	247		227	534	2466	451	86	1611	5149
Russia	4	3143	134	61	39	556	3937	101	31		4069	9102	627	1859	12	15669
Total exports to WCA	52	4303	264	179	855	999	6652	508	617	8300	16077	17196	2535	3658	4417	43883
as % of the total exports	28%	21%	38%	20%	22%	40%	23%	1%	5%	5%	6%	3%	3%	6%	7%	4%
China	1	2066	84	0	13	371	2535	3961	300	10020	16815		4178	392	1176	22561
India	39	13	1	0	9	26	88	333	158	2461	3039	5927		136	3592	12694
Turkey	6	401	12	140	160	162	881	1783	219	7200	10083	2822	657		166	13727

(continued)

Table B.5. Exports (FOB, $US millions) within Wider Central Asia as a Share of Total Regional Exports (2004) (*Continued*)

Exports to:	Exports (as reported by exporters) by:															
	AFG	KAZ	KGZ	TJK	TKM	UZB	CA	IRN	PAK	RUS	WCA	CHN	IND	TUR	UAE	Wider CA & neighbors
United Arab Emirates	4	280	198	0	124	0	606	398	982	482	2468	6842	6605	1139		17054
Total Exports to WCA plus main neighbors	103	7061	559	320	1161	1559	10763	6982	2275	28462	48482	32787	13976	5325	9351	109921
as % of the total exports	55%	34%	80%	35%	30%	62%	37%	17%	17%	17%	19%	6%	19%	8%	14%	10%
Total Exports (World)	185	20814	703	915	3810	2524	28951	40921	13284	166369	249525	593232	75384	62923	67087	1048152

Source: IMF Directions of Trade Statistics.

the wider Central Asia region is realizing the potential for beneficial exchange that this entails—the challenge is to make the required political commitments and compromises possible and sustainable.

Proposed New Transport Corridors

The above discussion explains why there has been much focus on new transport links between Central Asia and the Persian Gulf or Indian Ocean through Afghanistan. Attention has been concentrated on providing access to the new deep water port currently being built at Gwadar in Pakistan, as well as to the existing port of Bandar Abbas in Iran. In addition, Iran is developing a port to the east from Bandar Abbas at Chabahar, while Karachi remains, of course, Pakistan's main port and its commercial capital.

An ADB study (2005a) identified a total of 52 potential routes along the major North-South corridors to the above mentioned ports (including also Port Qasim just east of Karachi), and provided cost estimates for the construction and rehabilitation of these routes. The combination of different border crossing points into Afghanistan (at Hairatan [Uzbekistan], Shirkhan-Bandar [Tajikistan], and Aquina [Turkmenistan]) with different routes through Afghanistan explains the multiple alternatives. ADB also took the quality of road conditions along each corridor into account in making an estimate of investment costs and resulting reductions in vehicle operating costs, in order to obtain more precise estimates of economic returns for these investments.

The results of this study are summarized in Table B.6. These suggest that the benefits of investing in new road corridors through Central Asia are very significant indeed. Investments totalling an estimated US$5.6 billion would raise total trade by some 15 percent compared with the no-investment case, or by some US$12 billion, by 2010. In the same vein, as mentioned above should security and policy obstacles to rail and road transit through Afghanistan, Iran, and Pakistan be overcome, the southern rail link to Bandar-Abbas and the road link to Karachi would be highly competitive with northern and western routes to the Baltics and the Black Sea (Figure B.1).

Assumptions and Knowledge Gaps

The estimated gains from investments in transport reported above appear to be quite attractive. Indeed, they imply that the donor community should examine their current investment plans and make sure that they are coordinated along the major transport routes identified. With delays in road rehabilitation works in Afghanistan (particularly in the western part) bottlenecks along some major routes may remain and reduce the benefits of investments made further to the north or south along the corridors. Figure B.2 shows a map of all major highway projects in Afghanistan along with donor financing (and in most cases execution) responsibilities. As this map shows, highway reconstruction in Afghanistan has been divided among a number of different donors, and a fair amount of work has already been completed. The purely physical barriers to trade and transit with and through Afghanistan clearly have come down. For example, most of the North-South route from

Table B.6. Key Impact of Central-South Asian Road Corridors under Various Scenarios

Item	Base Case ($0)	20% Reduction in Traffic Flow ($1)	20% Reduction in Voc Savings ($2)	20% Reduction in Average truck load ($3)	20% Reduction in Traffic Flow, Voc Savings and Average Truck load ($4)
Combined incremental regional trade growth 2002–2010 (%)	160	129	155	113	90
Combined incremental regional transit trade growth 2002–2010 %	111	93	111	89	75
Corridor investment cost ($ million)	5639	5639	5639	5639	5639
Corridor investment as % of total investment	4.55	4.66	4.56	4.67	4.75
Annual travel cost saving/$ of investment 2010 ($)	0.31	0.25	0.25	0.31	0.20
Incremental annual GDP growth rate 2005–2010 (%)	0.43	0.35	0.42	0.34	0.28
Incremental annual GDP/$ of investment 2010 ($)	1.05	0.85	1.04	0.83	0.68
Incremental annual full time employment in 2010 (million)	1.86	1.50	1.85	1.48	1.20
Total incremental export growth 2002–2010 (%)	14	13	14	13	12
Total incremental import growth 2002–2010 (%)	16	15	16	15	14
Incremental revenue in 2010 ($ million)	910	863	908	863	827

Notes: Impact is due to corridor over without corridor.
Voc = vehicle operating cost
Source: Staff estimates; ADB (2005a).

Figure B.1. Trade-Transport Costs in Some Central Asian Republics

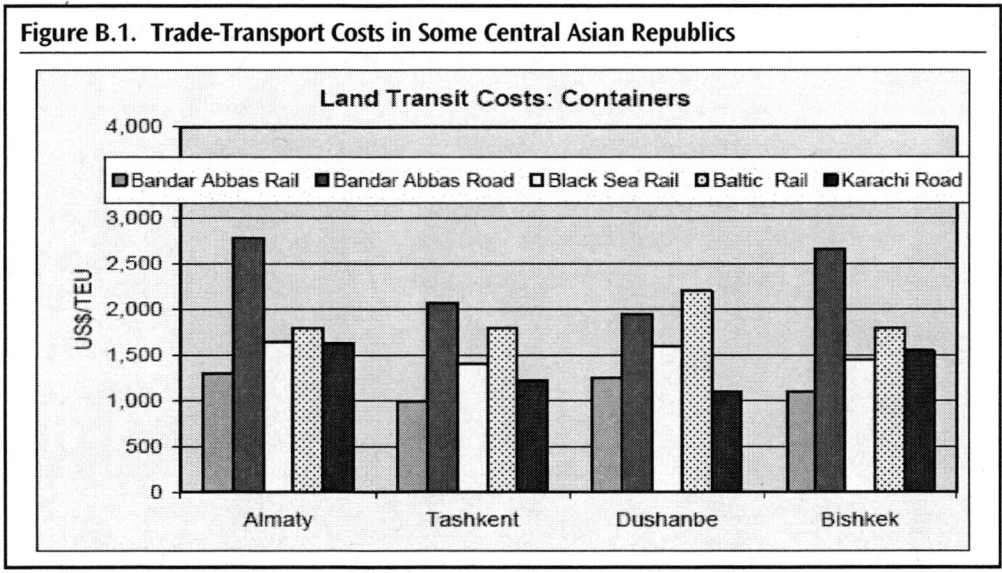

Source: World Bank (2004).

Khairatan on the Uzbekistan border through the Salang Pass and Kabul leading southeast to Peshawar in Pakistan, or alternatively going further south through Kandahar to Quetta (also in Pakistan), has been improved.

However, two important caveats need to be made regarding the estimated gains from investments in transport infrastructure. The first is that estimates of trade flows along new corridors generally assume that cost reductions will translate directly into higher trade along these routes. This may be true for intra-regional trade, and in particular for trade with and through Afghanistan from post-Soviet Central Asia. However, for transit trade, estimates should be made in relation to the cost of alternative routes. Unfortunately, so far no consolidated estimates exist of the cost of major inter-continental transport routes that would allow the attractiveness, say, of a route linking Moscow and Karachi through Tashkent and Kabul, to be compared to that of the alternative link Moscow–Baku–Tabriz–Persian Gulf. Such a broader study is of high priority, so that the benefits of upgrading transport routes for transit trade can be properly evaluated. What is known to date suggests that the potential for inter-regional transit through Central Asia should be evaluated with caution.

One additional implication of this caveat is that if intra-regional trade is the main target in the short run, routes might be dimensioned differently. For instance, the bridge currently being built across the Pandzh River between Tajikistan and Afghanistan will make a great contribution to reducing the former country's dependence on transit through Uzbekistan. However, it may be of less significance as a link in a longer North-South corridor, given that onward road links bypassing Uzbekistan inevitably must cross high mountain passes closed for several months of the year. Nonetheless, in generating new mutually beneficial trading opportunities between southern Tajikistan and northern Afghanistan, the bridge may soon start to have significant local benefits. Moreover, it may reduce the effectiveness of Uzbekistan's present policies sufficiently to induce changes. As such, investments like the Pandzh river bridge may be among the "bold strokes" that donors might support to unlock

Figure B.2. Major Highway Reconstruction and Rehabilitation Works in Afghanistan

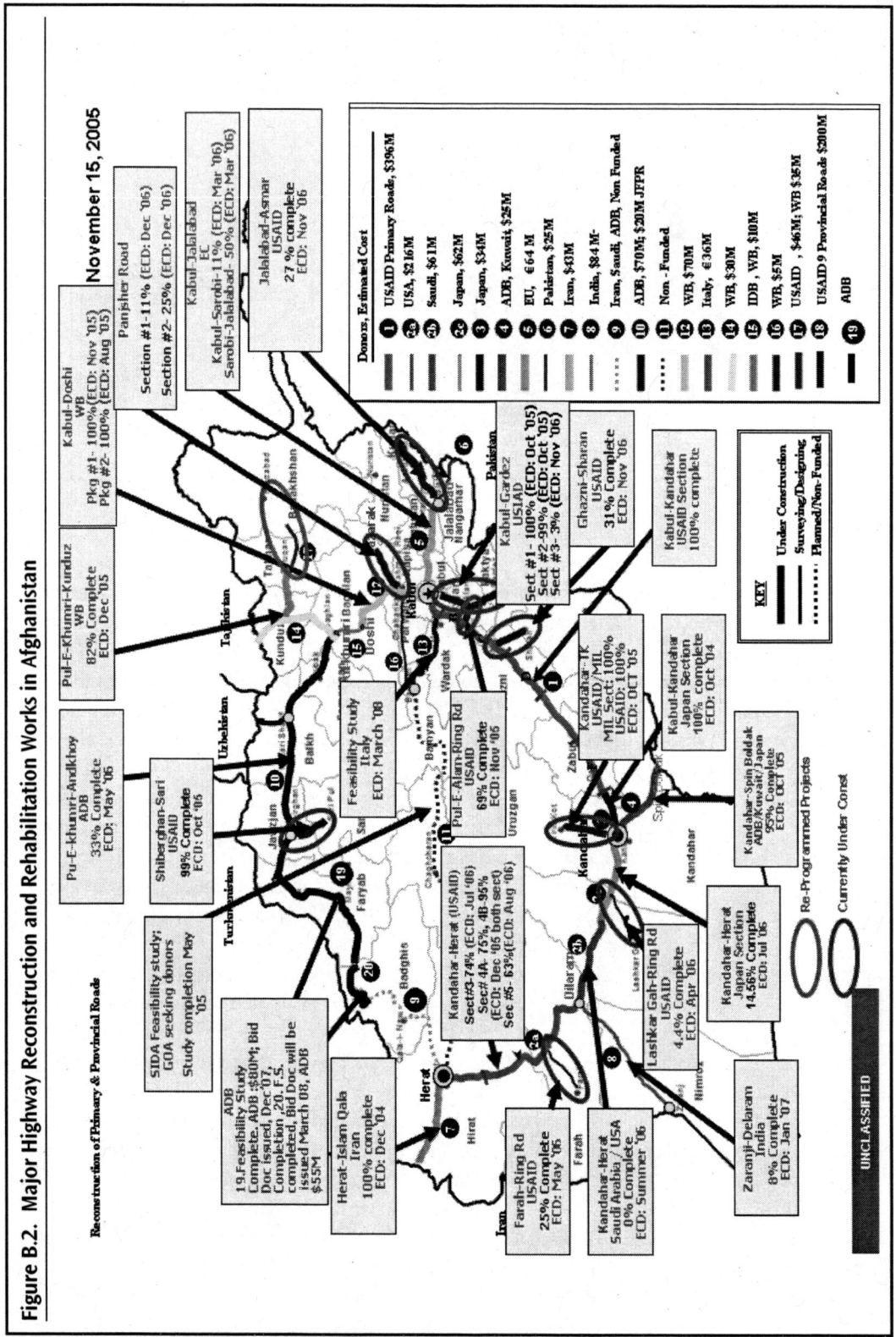

Source: Consultative Group for the Transport Sector, Afghanistan.

the regional cooperation agenda. Evaluating whether benefits are mainly local or have wider regional implications is important for donors to target their support appropriately.

The second caveat is that the estimates contained in Table B.6 and Figure B.1 depend on trade and transit facilitation measures being adopted by the countries of the region. Without such measures, the costs of informal payments and of time delays will continue to hamper both intra- and inter-regional trade and transit. This includes the further stabilization of Afghanistan, where the current security situation essentially acts like an additional tax on transport operators, who resort to paying "protection money" to local power-brokers to be granted safe passage. Security risks have also in the past delayed reconstruction efforts by donors. Appendix C deals in detail with the policy issues around trade and transport facilitation. For donors, this caveat implies that infrastructure investments and technical assistance for trade facilitation should be well-coordinated and sequenced, and focused along pilot corridors to leverage policy change and demonstrate its benefits. The identification of such pilot corridors is a priority for the donor community in the short run.

An additional knowledge gap is the need for a detailed study of the potential economic returns to investments and reforms in air transportation. The World Bank is presently undertaking a civil aviation study for post-Soviet Central Asia to address serious policy shortcomings, such as the lack of separation of regulatory from operational functions, restrictions on landing rights for foreign airlines which limit competition and unnecessarily increase costs, safety risks, and poor pricing and marketing. Moreover, while wider Central Asia would potentially benefit significantly from having an integrated air space given the high physical barriers to land transportation, the market is fragmented among several mostly state-owned airlines. Currently there are no direct flights between Tajikistan and Uzbekistan, Tajikistan and Turkmenistan, Turkmenistan and Kyrgyzstan, and only one flight per week between Turkmenistan and Kazakhstan. In Afghanistan, the situation is not much different. While such lack of connectedness is not uncommon in the developing world, it takes longer to fly by plane from Tashkent to Kabul (via Dubai, Delhi, or Almaty and Dushanbe) than from London, and the connectivity is poor. If business ties within the wider Central Asia region are to develop further, better integration of airline routes and opening up of regional air transport markets will be required.

Finally, it is important to recognize the role of the private sector in reducing transport and logistics costs. Few estimates are available on the cost increases due to the lack of real private sector competition in the freight forwarding business, the absence of functioning logistics centers (in particular in Afghanistan), etc. Appreciating the contribution the private sector can make to reducing transport costs requires involving private sector representatives in the discussions on transport and trade facilitation.

Short-run Recommendations

The above analysis suggests four areas in which progress could be made in the short term:

First, the donor community should complete the analytical work on transit corridors through the wider Central Asia region by extending the analysis of costs to a comparison of different transcontinental transit routes. There are no comparable cost estimates for long-distance transit through the region, so estimates regarding the potential increase in transit trade resulting from improved transportation and trade facilitation measures are necessarily imprecise. This includes the evaluation of the potential benefits of a railway link through Afghanistan, which while attractive to Afghanistan and potentially to Central Asia, would need to be justified by a detailed feasibility analysis. The last such study dates back to 1975.

Second, such a costing exercise could be combined with the development of a performance measurement system for the very same transport corridors, so that policy-induced bottlenecks can be clearly identified and raised at the appropriate bilateral or regional forums. Moreover, as logistics costs such as cargo handling, transhipment, and storage can account for a significant share of transport costs (and transport delays), it may be necessary to undertake a more detailed assessment of bottlenecks in this area, which has tended to receive inadequate attention in studies undertaken so far. The World Bank has recently supported the implementation of a performance measurement system along nine transport corridors from post-Soviet Central Asia, and is undertaking similar work for Afghanistan and Pakistan as part of its customs modernization projects in both countries.

One outcome of the proposed analytical work could be the designation of particular transit routes and border crossings as pilot projects for donor-assisted improvements in trade and transit facilitation along one or more rehabilitated corridors. The progress demonstrated could help catalyze improvements in other areas and more generally in trade and transit facilitation in the region.

Third, one implication of this analytical work might be to start considering construction of and donor financing for second-best transit corridors bypassing countries that have shown persistent reluctance to engage in a dialogue on trade and transit facilitation. At present, there are no reliable estimates of the potential economic returns to such investments, and it is hoped, of course, that in the meantime the political process of regional cooperation would progress sufficiently to make them unnecessary. The foregoing analysis suggests, however, that transit rents are considerable, amounting to some US$1,500–2,000 for the additional border crossing between Tajikistan and Uzbekistan and US$1,000 between the Kyrgyz Republic and Kazakhstan. It is clearly not realistic to consider major investments in transport corridors without a sober assessment of the likelihood for greater cooperation in border management, customs, transit arrangements and insurance, and mutual entry regulations for transport operators.

The fourth recommendation is to encourage the formation of forums of private transport operators, including truckers, freight forwarders, freight brokers, transport insurance companies, and so forth. These forums could develop recommendations for reducing entry barriers for private investors in the sector, and highlight key public investments that would stimulate private sector activity. In Kazakhstan this process has started through the Congress of Business Associations of Central Asia, and in Pakistan the private sector is part of the National Trade Facilitation Council. Other regional countries may wish to consider similar arrangements.

Improving Trade and Transit Facilitation

The prospects for expanding trade in the wider Central Asia region, including the significant potential benefits of improved transportation infrastructure along the main North-South corridors through Afghanistan, depend crucially on the adoption of better policies to promote trade and transit. This is a challenging agenda, as the discussion in this Appendix shows. Donors will need to sequence physical investments carefully to synchronize them with progress on the "soft" components of trade and transit facilitation and to ensure that financial assistance is used to leverage politically sensitive but economically essential policy reforms. Against this background, this Appendix makes some proposals for short-term measures that would signal commitment, generate immediate benefits, and through these benefits and by building confidence stimulate deeper reforms and larger-scale physical investments.

Obstacles to Trade and Transit

Different Trade Policy Regimes

At the origin of many of the obstacles hindering trade and transit lie the significant variations in trade policy regimes across the region (see Figure C.1). These differences in trade policies are reflected in policy-induced variations in prices of goods in the different national markets, in turn leading to incentives for shuttle traders to exploit these differences (Tables C.1 and C.2). However, it is interesting to note that the price differences between for example the Kyrgyz Republic and Uzbekistan are much smaller than would be implied by the combination of tariffs and excise duties imposed on many consumer goods

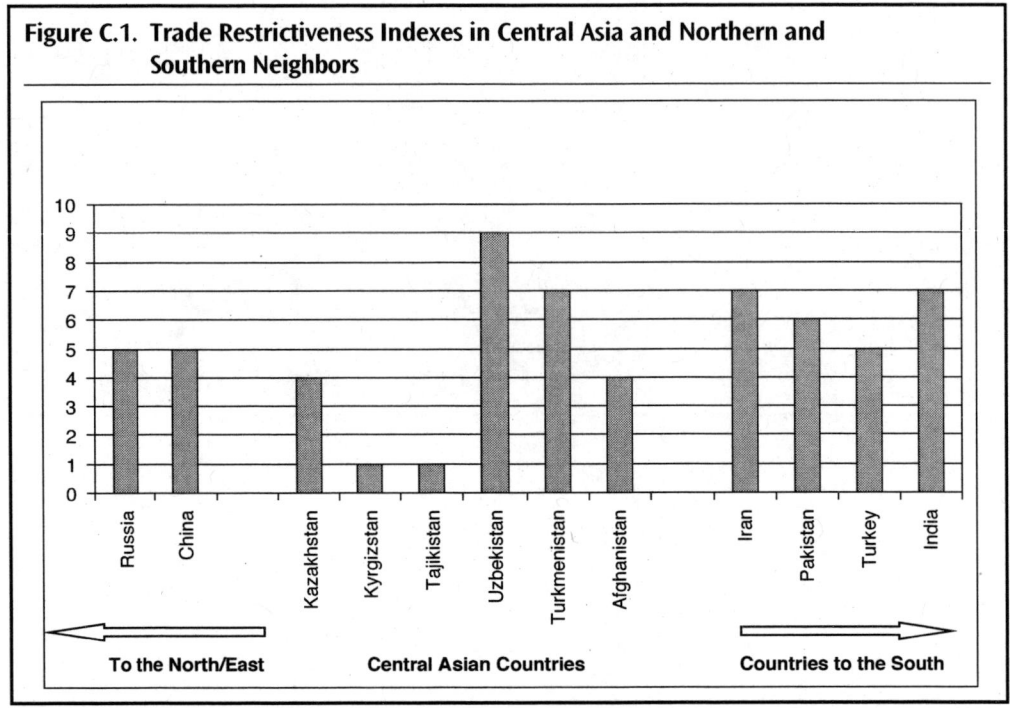

Figure C.1. Trade Restrictiveness Indexes in Central Asia and Northern and Southern Neighbors

imported into Uzbekistan, suggesting significant informal trade is taking place (Table C.1; see also Grafe, Raiser, and Sakatsume 2005).

While informal trade generates important employment opportunities in particular for poor people, it undermines revenue collection and creates significant difficulties for domestic producers, who instead of being protected face competition from informal imports which pay neither import duties nor domestic taxes.[20] Some governments therefore seek to suppress informal trade by making it more difficult to cross borders and in some cases, like Uzbekistan and Turkmenistan, placing restrictions on domestic wholesale and retail trade to raise entry costs for informal imports. But these policies affect not only small informal traders but formal traders as well. The fear of informal trade evading customs and other duties is also one of the main reasons for the high costs of transit trade, manifested in the requirement for escort services, failure to implement the TIR convention, and so forth. Harmonization of trade policies is likely to be needed if progress in other areas of trade and transit facilitation is to be sustainable.

Customs and Border Clearance Procedures

Crossing borders anywhere in the world is costly. In particular, commercial traffic often faces cumbersome formal documentation and registration requirements and lengthy delays before receiving clearance. Table C.3 illustrates some of the obstacles faced by traders wishing to clear goods through customs in Central Asia. Compared with their

---

20. Such complaints are heard frequently, for instance, from Uzbek and Pakistani businessmen.

Table C.1: Comparison of Prices for Main Consumer Durables in Tashkent, Shymkent, and Dushanbe

Commodity	Characteristics	Ratio of Tashkent/ Shymkent prices	Ratio of Tashkent/ Dushanbe Prices
Color TV	Daewoo 21T5 (21 inch screen)		1.07
Color TV	Daewoo 21Q1 (21 inch screen)		1.01
Color TV	Sony 21M80 (21 inch screen)		1.03
Color TV	Samsung 21Q3 (21 inch screen)	0.97	1.12
Color TV	Samsung 21D9 (21 inch screen)	0.97	0.98
VCR	Daewoo F54W		1.67
Music Center	Samsung 750 (3-VCD/ MP3CD Player, 4600W)	0.94	1.12
Music Center	Samsung (3-VCD/MP3CD, 3000W)	0.9	1.07
Refrigerator	Samsung SR-29NXB	1.29	1.12
Refrigerator	Sansybg RT-30MB	1.2	1.5
Refrigerator	Atlant 1700	1.23	1.04
Refrigerator	Atlant 1701	1.19	
Refrigerator	Atlant 1709	1.22	1.12
Gas-Stove	Gefest 3100/07	1.19	
Gas-Stove	Gefest 3100/00	0.95	
Gas-Stove	Gefest 1100/07	0.96	0.84
Gas-Stove	Gefest 1100/01	0.85	0.89
Air Conditioner	LG 12LH (Cooling/Heating)	1.2	0.95
Kettle	Tefal Vetesse	1.5	1.16
Dish Washer	Indesit WIL 105	1.14	1.03
Dish Washer	Ubdesut W43T	1.28	0.79
Microwave Oven	Sansung M 193SR	1.27	
Microwave Oven	Samsung CE2833NR	1.39	1.25

Source: World Bank survey of Spring 2004.

Table C.2. Average Absolute Price Disparities Between Country Pairs

Country Pairs	Kaz & Uzb	Kaz & Kyr	Kaz & Taj	Uzb & Taj	Kaz & Rus	Uzb & Kyr	Kyr & Taj
Price Disparity	59%	48%	43%	26%	23%	23%	19%

Note: the price disparities were calculated based on a range of country average prices for some 31 homogeneous imported and domestically produced goods. In each case the lowest prices were taken for 100 percent and the absolute price disparity was calculated. Prices for Russia were calculated on the basis of Samara and Omsk Prices (cities not far from Kazakh border).

Table C.3. Trading Across Borders

Region Or Economy	Documents for Export (number)	Signatures for Export (number)	Time for Export (days)	Documents for Import (number)	Signatures for Import (number)	Time for Import (days)
Europe & Central Asia	7	10	31	11	15	42
OECD: High income	5	3	12	6	3	14
South Asia	8	12	33	12	24	46
Uzbekistan	..	..	..	18	32	139
Kyrgyz Republic	..	..	..	18	27	127
Afghanistan	..	..	..	10	57	97
Kazakhstan	14	15	93	18	17	87
Iran	11	30	45	11	45	51
India	10	22	36	15	27	43
Pakistan	8	10	33	12	15	39
Russian Federation	8	8	29	8	10	35
Turkey	9	10	20	13	20	25
China	6	7	20	11	8	24
United Arab Emirates	6	3	18	6	3	18

Source: World Bank (2005c).

regional neighbors, Afghanistan and post-Soviet Central Asia clearly have some of the most time-consuming border procedures, and as the number of signatures and documents required for import clearance demonstrates, this is not just because of physical constraints.

A notable issue in all countries of wider Central Asia is the presence of several inspection and enforcement agencies at the border, who often act in an uncoordinated and highly discretionary manner. For instance, in Russia in 2004 up to 11 such enforcement agencies were active at the Russian-Finnish border, according to Finnish customs (Ojala 2005). A culture of control and red tape prevails among most enforcement agencies, leading to duplication and harassment. While customs codes are being reformed throughout the region, implementation may lag behind changes in primary legislation, leading to legal and procedural inconsistencies. This can occur even though Central Asian customs have comparatively low case loads and indicates the need for improved customs efficiency.

Trucking Fees, Visas, and Transit Facilitation

As reported in Appendix B, a large part of the estimated economic returns from new transportation routes come from increased transit trade potential. Of particular importance in this respect are improvements in the regulation of transit by road. Because of concerns over the evasion of import duties, governments often require trucks in transit to be escorted. Private escort services are expensive, costing between US$1,000–1,500 per truck for a crossing through Kazakhstan, and up to US$2,000 through Uzbekistan (these numbers include informal payments to the road police). Truckers usually prefer convoy systems (rather than the ambiguous "escort service"), for the following reasons: (i) greater security, (ii) no need to make a deposit for the duties (which is always difficult and takes a long time to get back), and (iii) absence of road police or other harassment. Convoys are escorted by Customs. Normally, there is one convoy per day, except in Tajikistan where delays of 2–3 days waiting for convoys to form are common.

In principle the TIR convention, which all post-Soviet countries are signatories to but which does not apply in Afghanistan, allows sealed trucks to transit unchecked to the final destination market. In practice this is not enforced, the number of TIR carnets issued is minimal (21,500 for the whole of Central Asia in 2003), and alternative insurance bonds are not available. Application of TIR is also hampered by the lack of modern trucks that would meet TIR requirements, except in Iran and Kazakhstan, where a reasonably modern fleet exists. It is often cumbersome and expensive for truckers to obtain visas (Table C.4), or as in the case of Afghan truckers wanting to operate in Pakistan or in Uzbekistan and Turkmenistan, outright impossible. Entry fees for truckers operating on foreign territory can add additional costs.[21]

Table C.4: Cost of Visas in Central Asian Republics, 2005 (In US dollars)				
	For CIS Nationals		**For Non-CIS Nationals**	
Country	**Single Entry**	**Multiple Entry**	**Single Entry**	**Multiple Entry**
Azerbaijan	0	0	40	250
Kazakhstan	Varies	Varies	70	210
Kyrgyz Republic	4	20	35	125
Tajikistan	7–8	60	30–60	150–350
Uzbekistan	4–6	30	60	250

Source: ADB (2005b).

The above obstacles create entry barriers against private trucking companies without the required connections with customs officials and the road police, who try to extract further rents along the way through checkpoints, and so forth. These are compounded in Afghanistan by security concerns in parts of the country, as well as levies by illegitimate authorities akin to "protection money" (perhaps not too different in their impact on transporters from police checkpoints in some other countries of the region), and in much of post-Soviet Central Asia by the absence of competitive private sector transport markets, with aging fleets and still dominant government ownership, leading to further rises in costs.

---

21. A particular problem appears to be that entry permits for truckers are issued on a reciprocal bilateral basis. Since there are considerably more demands for entry into Central Asia than demands by Central Asian road carriers for entry into other markets, truckers often have to purchase "empty" reciprocal permits, adding to the cost of these fees.

Benefits of Improved Trade and Transit Facilitation

One recent study estimates that the combined logistics and policy-induced costs to trade and transit add around 7–10 percent to final export and import prices in Central Asia along the existing routes through Russia, roughly the same order of magnitude as the direct transport-related costs alone (Ojala 2005). The same study suggests that while the direct transport-related costs of road shipment to Iran or Pakistan could be highly competitive, logistics costs of transit lead to it being significantly underutilized (see Appendix B).

Ojala (2005) estimates that the benefits of trade and transport facilitation measures that address the above obstacles could amount to a 10 percent increase in trade values. A study by the Asian Development Bank (2005b), which takes into account the combined benefits of improved transportation and trade facilitation, calculates the incremental trade value to be around 15 percent, or US$12 billion, for the wider Central Asia region as a whole. These gains are distributed relatively evenly between increased intra-regional trade and transit trade.

Another study (Raballand, Kunth, and Auty 2005) evaluates the quantitative gains of better trade and transport integration of wider Central Asia with major consumer markets in Europe and Asia. They argue that the high costs of road transportation, and the large economies of scale in rail transportation, have led to a distorted export structure, concentrated on bulk commodities with relatively low value/weight ratios, and that product diversification of trade would benefit dramatically from improved road transportation and rail freight forwarding services. In other words, relative costs of different modes of transport are locking in the production structure established under central planning and may be delaying necessary structural changes.

However, a strong word of caution is in order in relation to these estimates. For the short to medium term at least, increased long-distance transit trade through Afghanistan and most other Central Asian countries remains unlikely. The security situation continues to present a risk,[22] and—perhaps even more important—for transit trade to Russia, China, or Iran, alternative routes exist that do not face the same constraints. This is reflected in recent trends in regional trade (Appendix B).

Realistically, therefore, the outlook for long-distance trade and transit in the Wider Central Asia region in the short to medium term is modest. Informal traders are likely to be the first ones to benefit from greater security and improved transport links through Afghanistan, bringing consumer goods from the Gulf to Central Asia, and exploiting the continuing divergence in trade policies across the region. As for formal trade, this is likely to concentrate initially on trade routes into Afghanistan from Iran and Pakistan, and only in the second instance on transit trade through, to, and from post-Soviet Central Asia. One potential exception to this pattern is Tajikistan, which facing significant transit obstacles through Uzbekistan, may increasingly choose southern routes for its commerce, aided by

---

22. One should perhaps not overstate the security issue in Afghanistan. In most of Afghanistan, shippers are able to buy protection, and hence security is largely a cost rather than an uninsurable risk issue. It is interesting that actual losses of goods in shipment through Afghanistan are surprisingly low, which reflects the strength and effectiveness of the informal economy, including the regional trucking mafias, and informal arrangements between truckers and warlords etc. which allow transport to happen. However, such arrangements are no substitute for adequate modern trade and transit facilitation mechanisms and well-functioning logistics chains, which are essential for robust longer-term growth of exports and transit trade.

the expected completion of a major bridge across the Amu Darya River. The investment in transport links within Tajikistan from the South to Leninabad province in the North (in particular the construction of a year-round tunnel through the Anzob pass) would extend these links into the populated Ferghana valley. While this represents a great economic opportunity, it might add to the significant political tensions in the valley, resulting from contiguous borders between three countries with highly divergent trade policy regimes.

Proposals for Improved Trade and Transit Facilitation

The obstacles listed above do not lend themselves to a quick fix. The harmonization of trade policies, for instance, has taken other regions several decades to complete. Governance problems and limited government capacity will most likely result in a slow pace of improvements in trade and transit facilitation, and implementation is likely to continue to lag behind changes in formal laws and regulations. Mindful of these constraints, the recommendations below focus on the short run.

Transparent Performance Measurement to Help Bring to Bear the Lobbying Power of the Private Sector, Overcome Political Resistance, and Mobilize Donor Support

Politicians and donors generally find it easier to justify interventions and commit resources if a problem can be quantified, and if the results of specific interventions are reflected in measurable improvements. The World Bank has gained important experience in Southeastern Europe in developing a performance measurement system for trade facilitation. This involves regularly checking border crossing times, the number of irregularities discovered during inspections, incidents of corruption, etc. The information is collected from both public agencies and trucking businesses and put on a computer system for easy reference. At a regional conference on trade and transit facilitation in Central Asia in Bishkek (in March 2005), it was agreed that a similar performance measurement system should be developed for Central Asia, and the World Bank has begun this work. The meeting also established certain performance benchmarks for improvements in physical infrastructure and for the increase in regional trade volumes. Similar performance measurement systems are being developed as part of customs modernization projects in Afghanistan and Pakistan; it may be possible to link up these initiatives and obtain consistent performance measures for the planned trans-Afghan transport corridors.

Harmonization of Customs Legislation

The legal harmonization of customs codes has progressed relatively far in post-Soviet Central Asia, driven by WTO accession and convergence toward implementation of the Revised Kyoto Convention. New customs codes have been adopted in Kazakhstan, the Kyrgyz Republic, and Tajikistan, all modeled on the Russian code, while Uzbekistan and Turkmenistan are expected to adopt new codes during 2006 at the latest. As a result, the primary legislation is likely to be similar in these countries by next year, even if not identical. The compatibility with standards and procedures in place in Afghanistan, Iran, and Pakistan should not present a major obstacle. Under CAREC a customs coordination committee (CCC) has been created, and with membership in CAREC, Afghanistan could join the CCC, while the Economic Cooperation Organization could lead similar efforts with Iran and Pakistan. Technical assistance could be provided by donors to adopt compatible and simplified documentation requirements, as well as proper IT systems at customs.

Risk-based Approach to Border Control

Changes in primary customs legislation and customs procedures alone will not suffice. There is a broader issue here of changing from a culture of control, and persistent corruption, to a border control system based on risk mitigation and trade facilitation. This agenda has to be wider than just customs alone, involving border guards, the road police, and other inspection agencies (for example, phyto-sanitary or veterinary agencies). The short-run objectives should be to:

- At the national level, reduce the burden of controls and documentation as much as possible—on both sides of the border. In Pakistan, for instance, a National Trade Facilitation Committee has been formed, which includes all the agencies involved in the border clearance process, as well as private shippers associations, port authorities, public transport companies (Pakistan Railways, Pakistan International Airlines), Pakistan Bankers Association, and others.
- Bilaterally or regionally, ensure that border clearance standards of one country are accepted by the other country so that transit traffic is checked and controlled only once. While the benefits of harmonization would be greater the more countries are involved, bilateral harmonization is also desirable (and perhaps more feasible). A first step if closer cooperation is not feasible, presently being explored between the Kyrgyz Republic and Uzbekistan, is the simple exchange of information, which will become easier as customs adopt modern IT systems. Donors should adapt their assistance to customs and border agencies in ways that will fit into a wider regional approach, once this becomes feasible at a later date.

Trucking Fees, Visas, Transit Insurance

At the last Trade Policy Committee meeting of CAREC, the issue of high trucking and transit fees was addressed, and as initial steps it was agreed that member countries would work to:

- Reduce the charges for transit convoys and the list of goods subject to such convoys.
- Abolish all other fees for the entry or transit of foreign road carriers.
- Ensure full implementation of the TIR convention among those CAREC members who have adhered to it (Afghanistan and China have not, but the latter is likely to join soon).
- Reduce the cost of visas for truckers.
- Take measures to eliminate unofficial payments to road police and other inspection bodies inside countries.

As indicated earlier, the above issues can be addressed at the national, bilateral, and regional levels, with the highest benefits likely to flow from coordinated multilateral action. However, several subregional initiatives would appear to make immediate sense:

- The re-introduction of a visa-free travel regime for the post-Soviet Central Asian republics, ideally under the umbrella of the Eurasian Secretariat for Economic Cooperation (EurASEC). This would allow the development of a subregional road carriers market and help address the issue of aging truck fleet stock and limited private sector entry in some of the post-Soviet Central Asian countries. It would also allow EurASEC to negotiate a single visa regime with Afghanistan, Iran, and Pakistan.
- Technical assistance on the implementation of TIR within EurASEC, including training of customs officials, and random checks on compliance with TIR rules.
- Creation of an association of Central Asian road carriers to promote policy reform, self-policing of compliance with TIR principles, and naming and shaming of violators.[23]
- Development of a specific transit insurance agreement through Afghanistan, perhaps underwritten by donor or bilateral assistance to promote trans-Afghan transit routes in the absence of TIR.

Trade Policy Harmonization and the Treatment of Small Informal ("Shuttle") Traders

Perhaps the biggest obstacle to trade and transit facilitation remains the great variation in protection levels across the region. The arbitrage gains are large enough to make governments in the more protective countries suspicious of transit commerce, but more generally of significant cross-border movements of goods and people. The evident solution here would be to reduce tariffs and in particular other tax-related barriers such as excises on imports (which can reach up to 100 percent in Turkmenistan and Uzbekistan) to levels that reduce the incentives for contraband. This would lead to increased official trade flows, higher customs revenues, and more effective protection of the domestic market. There is some hope (and expectation) that Uzbekistan's recent application to join EurASEC could provide the necessary leverage to start a process of trade liberalization in that country, which would be very beneficial not just for its own economy but for all of its neighbors. Yet, the process is likely to be slow, as Uzbekistan to date remains committed to its model of import substitution-based industrialization, and it is unclear what additional leverage EurASEC members could bring to bear on this issue.

In the absence of political will to consider general trade policy reforms and harmonization, countries might aim for pilot solutions to formalize existing informal trade. One such solution could be the creation of cross-border trading zones. Informal traders could be granted access to specific markets across the border for an entry fee (that includes any domes-

---

23. While in principle, TIR trucks are sealed and the seal can only be broken upon arrival in the destination market, there are anecdotal reports of trucks driving to the destination market with the seal unbroken, then breaking the seal and re-entering the transit country with the truck still fully loaded. This practice of re-export is prevalent in particular between Afghanistan and Pakistan, and between Uzbekistan and its other post-Soviet Central Asia neighbors.

tic sales or value added taxes). Commerce would be restricted to individual traders taking no more than what a person or a small vehicle can carry. Such markets could generate significant fee revenue; allow close supervision of the movements of shuttle traders in a circumscribed border zone, thereby alleviating security concerns; and effectively reduce smuggling. The approach could be extended to formal traders as well, and would allow the host countries to capture some of the arbitrage rents presently accruing to middlemen and shuttle traders. Uzbekistan, for instance, has lost the pre-eminence of the bazaars of Tashkent and Andijon to rival bazaars in Shymkent (Kazakhstan) and Osh/Kara-Su (Kyrgyz Republic). By creating delineated import zones around the border, Uzbekistan might succeed in relocating some wholesale trade into its own borders. Interestingly, plans have surfaced that foresee possible construction of such a bazaar on the Uzbek side of Kara-Su.

At what level should entry fees for the border zone be set? The total fee should be lower than present arbitrage gains to provide an incentive for shuttle traders to go formal. For example in the case of Uzbekistan, with domestic VAT of 20 percent and present average arbitrage gains in the range of 15–30 percent, the maximum total entry fee should probably be no more than 30–40 percent of the value of goods imported. This is much lower than the present 70 percent charged by Uzbekistan for shuttle traders (which evidently few pay). The impact of creating such preferential conditions for shuttle traders in lowering protective barriers against domestic competition would probably be relatively small, while the benefits for traders would be large. A similar regime might be designed for Afghanistan's trade with Iran and Pakistan.

Other Measures

Export financing and insurance are severely underdeveloped across the region. An interesting example of a short-run measure to promote regional trade in this respect comes from Iran. In November 2004 the Government of Iran authorized the Exports Guarantee Fund of Iran (EGFI) to extend insurance cover on the risk of nonpayment of loans to any Iranian bank which is willing to provide credit for exports to Afghanistan, as long as the loan approval is contingent on down payment of 15 percent of the contract's value, paid by the Afghan trade partner. The coverage limit for Afghanistan was initially set at $50 million, to be increased incrementally in the future. Similar arrangements might be explored for other bilateral trading relationships.

More generally, there is a large potential role to be played by the private sector in lowering trade and transport costs. However, the transport industry in many countries remains state-dominated, and where private operators exist in the region, they are often under-capitalized, use outdated equipment, and thus fail to cater effectively to the needs of intra-regional or transit trade. Donors could provide technical assistance to advise governments in the region on priorities in the development of a more efficient private transport and logistics services market. Given the lack of private financing, multilateral investors such as IFC and EBRD would be well-suited to modernize existing transport operators and invest in logistics centers such as modern warehouses and transshipment facilities.

In addition, donors might consider financial measures to support reforms in the sensitive trucking sector. In countries such as Afghanistan and Tajikistan, domestic financial markets may not be sufficiently developed to finance the required investments. One proposal for consideration would be the creation of a donor-supported trust fund for the modernization of the trucking fleet in Central Asia. Access to funding would be for both private and public sector operators but contingent on governments committing to reduce entry barriers, implement the TIR convention, and agree to basic technical standards such as freight load limits, emission standards, and so forth.

Leveraging Reform

As this list of short-term recommendations demonstrates, trade and transport facilitation is a huge agenda for the region. While it is often regarded as one of the key challenges for regional cooperation, the above list of recommendations includes several measures that countries can implement on their own. As with trade policy, the benefits from multilateral and coordinated reforms are higher, but the welfare gains from easing trade and transit for the country carrying out reforms are almost always positive, even if the distributional implications within the country are rarely neutral. The role of donors in this environment should be to try and maximize leverage for reform. This can be done by:

- Sequencing investments in physical infrastructure so that they reward countries that have undertaken efforts in the policy area as well. In some cases, physical investments may increase the benefits of policy reform by enough to create leverage even without conditionality. In either case, donors should be explicit about the links between investments and policy reform, all the while being realistic in their expectations.
- In cases where no breakthrough seems imminent and small confidence-building steps seem to make little progress, alternative transport routes, bypassing countries that are not seriously attempting to remove policy- and institution-based bottlenecks, might be considered to build up additional leverage. Such routes should be costed but only embarked upon if the returns are sufficiently high to be acceptable even if the other country were to give up its non-cooperative position relatively soon after project completion.

References

Ahmad, Masood, and Mahwash Wasiq. 2004. *Water Resource Development in Northern Afghanistan and its Implications for Amu Darya Basin.* World Bank Working Paper No. 36. Washington, D.C.: The World Bank.

Asian Development Bank (ADB). 2005a. "Report on the Economic Impact of Central-South Asian Road Corridors." Prepared for the Transport Committee of CAREC.

———. 2005b. "Central Asia Regional Cooperation in Trade, Transport and Transit." Paper prepared for the Trade Policy Committee of CAREC.

British Petroleum (BP). 2005. *Statistical Review of World Energy 2005.*

Grafe, Clemens, Martin Raiser, and Toshiaki Sakatsume. 2005. "Beyond the Border: Reconsidering Regional Trade in Central Asia." EBRD Working Paper, forthcoming.

Kaufman, Daniel, Art Kraay, and Massimo Mastruzzi. 2005. "Governance Matters IV: Governance Indicators for 1996–2004." Draft.

Limao, N., and A. Venables. 1999. "Infrastructure, Geographical Disadvantage and Transport Costs." *World Bank Economic Review* 15:451–479.

McKellar, Landis, Andreas Worgotter, and Julia Worz. 2000. "Economic Development Problems of Landlocked Countries." Transition Economic Series N14. Institute for Advanced Studies, Vienna.

Ojala, Lauri. 2004. "Tajikistan: Transport and Trade Facilitation." Background paper, Processed.

———. 2005. "Review of Inter-Regional Trade and Transport Facilitation in Europe and Central Asia Region, South Asia Region and East Asia and Pacific Region." Processed.

Raballand, Gael. 2003. "The Determinants of the Negative Impact of Land-Lockedness on Trade: An Empirical Investigation Through the Central Asian Case." *Comparative Economic Studies* 45:520–536.

Raballand, Gael, Antoine Kunth, and Richard Auty. 2005. "Central Asia's Transport Cost Burden and Its Impact on Trade." *Economic Systems* 29(1):6–31.

Stone, Jack. 2001. *Infrastructure Development in Landlocked and Transit Developing Countries.* United Nations Conference on Trade and Development.

United Nations. 2001. "World Economic and Social Survey." New York.

———. 2003. "Transit Transport Issues in Landlocked and Transit Developing Countries." New York.

United Nations Office on Drugs and Crime (UNODC). 2003. *The Opium Economy in Afghanistan: An International Problem.* New York: United Nations.

World Bank. 2004a. "Trade and Regional Cooperation between Afghanistan and its Neighbors." Washington, D.C.

———. 2004b. *Central Asia: Regional Electricity Export Potential Study.* Washington, D.C.

———. 2005a. *Afghanistan—State Building, Sustaining Growth, and Reducing Poverty.* Washington, D.C.

———. 2005b. *Aviation Study for Central Asia. Inception Report.* Washington, D.C.

———. 2005c. *Doing Business Around the World.* Washington, D.C.

———. 2005d. *Enhancing Gains from Migration in Eastern Europe and Central Asia.* Washington, D.C.

Eco-Audit

Environmental Benefits Statement

The World Bank is committed to preserving Endangered Forests and natural resources. We print World Bank Working Papers and Country Studies on 100 percent postconsumer recycled paper, processed chlorine free. The World Bank has formally agreed to follow the recommended standards for paper usage set by Green Press Initiative—a nonprofit program supporting publishers in using fiber that is not sourced from Endangered Forests. For more information, visit www.greenpressinitiative.org.

In 2005, the printing of these books on recycled paper saved the following:

Trees*	Solid Waste	Water	Net Greenhouse Gases	Electricity
463	21,693	196,764	42,614	79,130
"40" in height and 6-8" in diameter	Pounds	Gallons	Pounds	KWH